COLTRANE IN A CADILLAC

COLTRANE IN A CADILLAC

Robbie Coltrane with Graham Stuart

FOURTH ESTATE · London

First published in Great Britain in 1993 by Fourth Estate Limited
289 Westbourne Grove London W11 2QA

A catalogue record for this book is available from the British Library.

ISBN 1 85702 120 7

Design by Fielding Rowinski
Printed in Great Britain by Clays Ltd, St Ives Plc

Dedicated with love and thanks to Ed Sholokian, without whom this book would most certainly not have been written.

And to Ben Hamper and all the rivetheads, without whom this journey might have been made on a bicycle.

Contents

—David Juniper—

Chapter One

Los Angeles, California

There are only two choices for a man with a Cadillac obsession: go and give a shrink fifty quid an hour for the rest of his life, or get hold of a Caddy and drive it from Los Angeles to New York. I've never been totally convinced by psychiatry. It was time to have a Great Adventure.

Cars have been a fascination for me since I built the Coltrane Convertible out of Meccano at the age of ten, and I have been deconstructing and driving them ever since. The great advantage of rebuilding old cars compared to, say, collecting stamps or making matchstick models of Chartres Cathedral is that you can't get on a Penny Black and cruise the Strip. This was an opportunity for me to enjoy my obsession and at the same time see what was left of American culture before the whole Union became a theme park. I've always had an affinity with America and, like most Glaswegians, I was brought up with the faint suspicion that New York was just like Glasgow, only more so. My head was filled with the images of America I had collected from a lifetime of loving its movies, books, and music. A 3,500-mile road crossing of the country would tell me if any of my American dreams were near the mark.

I'd been dreaming about a journey like this since I was a wee boy. While other short corduroyed Scots lads were scoring the winning goal for Scotland in the World Cup final or finding themselves trapped all night in the Tunnocks Caramel Wafer factory (oh dearie me…) I was gripping a steering wheel twice my size seemingly made out of the same stuff as Granny's false teeth while trying not to be dazzled by a dashboard like the Golden Mile at Blackpool (with an ashtray in the middle, of course). Mile after mile of two-lane black-top was being sucked under the bonnet (or was I flying?). It always gave me strange feelings which I didn't come to understand until later. Like the ones you got on the beach when all the girls had very few clothes on.

Now, many years later, those nice television people had actually listened to my ramblings and the dream was about to become something more tangible, nay drivable…

It was just after 3 pm Pacific time on Sunday, October 18th as I flew in over the never-ending but always neat sprawl of Greater Los Angeles. I felt lagged already (those free cocktails always lag one, non?) as we descended from the brilliant blue sky into heavy cloud which left the town looking a dull mud colour that you never see on *Baywatch*. Somewhere down there in the geometrically irritating suburban mammoth that is Los Angeles was a person who held the key to my dream. All I had to do was find the key, and the ignition it fitted, and we would be in business. "We" being myself and a film crew. (I've always liked to keep a record of important moments in my life.)

I left LAX and headed for my hotel, alone in a car with my thoughts, a cameraman, sound man, director, and a driver anxious to give me advice. The only valid suggestion he had was to "have a good day". I was trying but I couldn't help but feel a bit concerned about the challenge I had set myself. "Los Angeles," I had exclaimed during one of those occasions television people call Programme Development meetings and I call going for a drink, "Los Angeles is the centre for Classic Cadillac collectors. I'll find the car we need in a couple of days." I checked the typed schedule in my pocket to confirm that my confidence had been contagious: "Arrive Los Angeles, Sunday; Buy car; Depart Los Angeles, Wednesday". I had a couple of phone numbers and forty-eight hours to find a two-ton Jezebel. A devil-may-care smile played on my lips but I noticed that no-one in the crew smiled back. This show was now officially on the road.

A hint of ozone pierced the carbon monoxide as the car turned onto Ocean Avenue in Santa Monica. Hopeless romantic that I am, I had decided to begin the trip staying in a small hotel on the ocean front so that I really could say the journey was coast to coast. The Georgian Hotel was a white Thirties block which until recently had been an old folk's home. Some of the previous residents had miraculously survived the transformation, pushing the average age in the dining room to around the eighty mark. Still, it was a fine hotel, particularly if you liked to have your food cut up for you.

Santa Monica, with its gaudy pier, tall palms and wide beach looked exactly like you wanted California to be. The Georgian sat contemplating the Pacific across a palm-tree-lined avenue which fell sharply away down to a half-mile-wide expanse of tarmac and sand before the ocean. Nipping out of the hotel for a paddle would be an all-day adventure. Just one block up from the hotel was a plaque marking the end of the most celebrated road in America, Route 66 from Chicago to Los Angeles (at 2,448 miles considerably shorter than the journey I was about to make), and the view of tropical splendour here sums up why it was a route worth getting your kicks on. California looked like paradise, which I'm sure it was, if your idea of heaven was noncing about in a pair of "Hey look at *my* genitals" Lycra shorts. I personally was in my "Please, Robbie, put them away" lightweight travelling suit, so called because even leaving Sketchleys passers-by ask, "Where the hell has that been?"

As you strolled on the beach at Santa Monica in the bright sun watching (enviously) the perfect bodies that seem to live on Evian water and perhaps the (very) occasional Häagen Dazs, it was hard to believe that six hours later the same dreamy arcades would be full of people stuffing their faces (and veins) with every drug known to man.

The search for the car would begin the next day. I was a proud member of the Cadillac/LaSalle Owners Club and the boys and girls who shared a love of Detroit's finest had given me several suggestions about the best place to buy the right car. In the meantime I had a chance to experience some traditional (ie "Established since August") Santa Monican cuisine at a restaurant in the shiny pedestrian precinct a couple of blocks from the hotel. This was also an opportunity to get to know the small band of seven desperate men, and one woman, who would be dogging my every step for the next five weeks or so. You know the kind of small talk: "Hello, how do you do, you're not as funny as Alexei Sayle, are you, fatty?" Preliminary investigation quickly threw up one crucial fact: not only had none of them ever had any kind of relationship with an old car but at the mention of the idea their eyes glazed over. I felt a chill as my jet-lagged mind's eye played a vivid image of a wounded Cadillac surrounded by eight helpless faces, all looking at me. I tried to remember if I had packed my boiler suit. I was pretty sure I was going to need it.

First we had to find the car. Everyone I asked about buying a Cadillac in California said go and see Frank Corrente. His address was recommendation enough: Frank Corrente's Cadillac Corner, 7614 Sunset Boulevard, Hollywood. I adjusted my posing shades, called a cab, and first thing Monday morning I was strolling off the fabled street into a small sales lot, crammed with Cadillacs. Fifteen feet above my head strands of the blue and silver tinsel so loved by American car salesmen rattled in the light Californian breeze. A man emerged from a Portacabin which seemed marooned in a sea of cars and as he approached sunlight flashed from a metal object dangling beneath his open shirt. There could never be any doubt about what Frank Corrente did for a living.

. . . .

This was Arthur Daley with a suntan, looking the look and talking the talk of an archetypal used-car salesman; although anyone with a yard full of Cadillacs is a quality person in my book. Frank listened to my request for an early Fifties Cadillac Convertible which would make it to New York and beyond and led me to a '52 Convertible painted in Doctor-Who-alien green. The car was in worse shape than I was. The chrome was marked and corroded in places, the soft top was rotted and torn, the front wings were three inches further back than nature intended, and I looked forward to Frank's spiel with some interest. In fact, his strategy was excellent, leading with the faults, quickly of course, then hitting me with pure, undiluted sales talk. "This car has had one careful owner and is perfect mechanically. This car runs smooth," he said, with the precision of a man who might just have used this line before. "My watch makes more noise than that motor." I could have kissed him. Frank wanted $29,000 for the whispering Caddy, plus $500 for the new roof, and around $3,000 for the paint job. Even if I gave him the cash right then the car would not be ready for a week, five days more than the schedule allowed. I made my excuses and left with the Corrente patter machine running on all cylinders behind me.

"Some people think I grow these cars, but it takes a lot of work to find them. Believe me, the money's right on this car, the price is definitely right. If it was perfect it would be fifty grand. Just say the word, close your eyes, and it'll be done..." I said the best word I could think of in the circumstances. Cheerio.

The next address I had was out in the San Fernando Valley. California Dream Cars in Van Nuys looked nothing on the outside, a low-rise industrial unit in a boring back street, but through the door I found the proverbial Sweetie Shop. Fifty or sixty Classic cars glittered in the fluorescent light and for a moment I wasn't sure where to start. On my left sat not one, but two, of the Ford Mustangs built by Carol Shelby for racing in the early Sixties. They looked mean and powerful and all that was missing was Steve McQueen. Superb cars and rarer than rocking-horse droppings, but sadly not quite what I was looking for. To the right a

stunning light-blue 1956 Lincoln Continental; behind it, a matching pair of Cadillac Convertibles. His and hers, if you so wished. I walked down the highly polished rows of cars and slowly the truth dawned on me: California Dream Cars and I had radically different approaches to the preservation of Classic cars. They took cars and completely rebuilt every single detail of them, usually finishing with a paint job the colour of a tart's handbag. This was a place for rock stars and hairdressers to buy the right ornament for their well-manicured lawn. Owner Bob Petricca tried his very best to sell me a gleaming red Cadillac Eldorado for $50,000, but if I wanted to look like Jayne Mansfield I would have the operation, thank you. The search had to go on.

Whenever students of automotive history meet hushed reference is often made to Bugatti and the legendary Schlumphf brothers who owned a mystical shed where Kubla Khan decreed that Molsheim's marvels would rest resplendent. A similarly mystic tale had reached my ears of one Ed Sholokian whose Californian Xanadu was said to bristle and shimmy with Detroit's delights. Bible, or *Hemmings Motor News* as it is more prosaically known, in hand, I made a lonely pilgrimage north to the foothills of the San Gabriel mountains and the hamlet of Sylmar. The opening of a humble gate revealed a yard, but this was no ordinary yard. It was cluttered with old cars and parts, but when my eye caught a Forties Cadillac ambulance and a Cadillac hearse (which I most certainly *would* be seen dead in) I knew instinctively *"this is the place"*. I rang the bell and watched as a door slid up to let the dazzling Southern Californian sun illuminate a gloomy warehouse. I felt like Howard Carter entering Tutankhamun's tomb for the first time. If someone had told me then that I had died and gone to heaven, I would not have argued. Everywhere I looked there was a Cadillac, each one sweeter than the last. It was like a dream I used to have, but in that I always used to wake up just as my hand touched the first car. Now I was caressing, even climbing into, magnificent Cadillacs and nobody was waking me up.

Ed Sholokian, as you may imagine, was no ordinary collector. Fourteen years ago he bought a 1947 Cadillac, spent some time doing it up, and

169 cars later had the largest privately owned Cadillac collection in the world. I was gazing at the sixty or so cars he kept in the warehouse which also housed his T-shirt printing business. In the old days that business used to take up most of the floor space but now the long tables where the shirts were printed were crammed into one corner, almost overrun by an army of glittering Cadillac cars and parts. And what cars! Ed always had a hankering for Classic Forties cars and his favourite was a stunning 1940 Model 62 four-door in beige, with running boards, dual-side spare-tyre mounts and a sun visor. It was the sort of car you could imagine Barbara Stanwyck giving Fred MacMurray a hard time in, beautiful, but not my personal cup of Java. A bit overblown, if you get my drift. For me the peak of Cadillac Style was when they stopped trying to be European. Raymond Loewy started the move towards unique American design with his Pennsylvania streamlined locomotives, while Harley Earl at General Motors used echoes of the new aerodynamic monoplanes of the USAF to drag cars futuristically away

from the coachbuilt pretensions of the Thirties. I think Earl's finest work came in the early- to mid-Fifties and, luckily, Ed had collected most of the Forties models he wanted after a few years, so had to move on to the next decade.

Ed Sholokian was a short, thickset man in his late fifties with a taste for Hawaiian shirts and a love of talking about cars. I liked him right away as he quickly introduced himself (with the kind of grip that has lifted a few transmissions in its time), then spent considerably more time introducing each of the cars around us: the car formerly owned by

Tyrone Power, the car driven by Bette Midler in *Risky Business*, a '49 which belonged to singer Al Jarreau. Ed's collection, it turned out, was an extraordinary labour of love which had never been intended for sale and was not even on show to the public. Just recently Ed had taken the decision to accept offers on his precious hoard of automobile history to give himself more time in his future retirement, and it came as no surprise that he thought he might have just what I was looking for.

If Rita Hayworth had been built in Detroit (and I've always had my suspicions) this is what she would have looked like. Curvaceous, naturally, but so well-proportioned that you could not imagine changing one detail without spoiling it. A 1951 Series 62 Cadillac Coupe Convertible, in glorious black with drop-dead gorgeous chrome-work and an ivory-white top over a burgundy Fleetwood interior, they did not get sweeter than this. I tried to play it cool with Ed and with only a slight quaver in my voice asked him to name his price. Thirty grand was his estimate, a lot less than the car would be worth in perfect nick but still a trifle more than I had in my purse. We had a full and frank discussion and ten minutes later she was mine for $25,000, Ed having admitted that there were several problems on the car he felt he should sort out. Unfortunately, I needed the car tomorrow so there would not be time to do all those jobs before we headed for New York. What the hell, it would be a pleasure handling any hiccups from this baby. Besides, I had my toolbox with me.

Late that Tuesday afternoon I drove out of Ed Sholokian's place in a car I had dreamed about owning for more years than I care to think about. The sun bounced happily off every shining inch of body and chrome, and the muscular V8 power plant under the hood pulled us effortlessly down the San Diego Freeway at 65 mph. Ed had done what he could in the few hours since I had bought the car, but he warned me that there were potential problems ahead on such a long journey with a vehicle which had not been completely overhauled. I found it hard to get wound up by thoughts of an aged six-volt electrical system and an engine which needed new mounts as the wind tugged at my hair and I blew the deep two-tone horn, just for the hell of it. She was running sweet as a nut and obviously enjoying being noticed by everyone on the freeway. When Americans saw it they just said, "Nice car!" which was a pleasant change from, "My Dad had one of those, and sold it for ten quid in 1974. I wish I had hung onto it now. I bet that car's worth a million pounds now," that I was used to in Britain.

I was now on schedule, much to the delight of the *Coltrane in a Cadillac* crew who were celebrating the coming together of the two key elements in their documentary series, as though the whole show was in the can. They seemed to be discounting the other part of their programme equation which, as I recalled, was a 3,500-mile drive across America through a complete range of geographical and meteorological challenges. A doddle, apparently.

There was one thing I wanted to do before setting out on this ultimate car drive: go for a drive in my car. I had bought a Cadillac in California and there was no way I was leaving the Golden State before I had cruised Los Angeles in my new motor. So, part of the first day's travel was an antidote to sitting in the back of a beaten up Chevvy taxi being shouted at in Romanian by someone who doesn't know where Sunset Boulevard is (my usual experience in LA). The first thing I noticed was that people got out of my way and of course I exploited this out-of-character politeness mercilessly. This has never been an instinctively "After you, old chap" city.

First I headed south, to Venice Beach where I think the wackiness and zaniness is all a bit predictable, then east on Santa Monica Boulevard towards Beverly Hills. As I drove down Beverly Drive with its rows of manicured palm trees (imported from Egypt) fringing the stately piles of the rich and famous I recalled the stories of armoured personnel carriers guarding these streets at the height of the LA riots. The rioters never did make it into Beverly Hills because they were too busy destroying their own areas and doing a billion dollars' worth of damage to a city already torn apart by economic and social strife. Things weren't what they used to be in California which had a massive budget deficit, rising

unemployment, and a shifting and potentially explosive ethnic mix. You could still take your poodle for a manicure in Beverly Hills but on the other side of the town there was drastic deprivation and suffering. I had a strange relationship with this town because of the job I do. I had to come here for work but I didn't particularly enjoy being here. The best piece of advice I was given about surviving as an actor in LA was that you must not be seen out anywhere after 9.30 pm. This is a town where people making films start work at 5.30 am, so a late night announces unemployment very clearly to your fellow members of the industry – never good for one's credibility down the Polo Lounge.

It was time to hit the road. I had worked out a basic route to New York which ran through key cities and places I was interested in on the way, but the plan was to point the car east every day and see where we got to. Some people were worried that a 3,500-mile drive behind the wheel all the way might be a wee bit too much of a challenge for an old fart (that's me – no-one would insult the car), but I swiftly disabused them of that nonsense. I'd wanted to do a drive like this since I was seventeen and I was not going to let this trip ever become *Coltrane in a* "Actually love, I went by chauffeur-driven limo but they'll never know the difference at home, ha ha" *Cadillac*. How I suffer for my art.

The first section of the trip was one of the classic American journeys: 272 miles through the Mojave Desert from Los Angeles to Las Vegas, city of high rollers and low morals. I happened to have heard the statistic that the second highest cause of accidental death in Vegas was bondage games that had gone horribly wrong so it was with a certain sense of anticipation that I settled into the warm, taut, inviting leather for the drive. It was late afternoon as I eased my way out onto the teeming Interstate and headed east out of Los Angeles. The oppressive noise and air of Los Angeles suddenly evaporated as the freeway carved a path through the San Gabriel mountains. I couldn't help thinking that convertible cars were built for trips like this. The air I was cruising through had a positively velvet texture as the sun did its best to rid me of my fetching nightclub tan. The road stretched for miles in a straight line and the Cadillac was going like a well-upholstered rocket. I felt like a guy in a movie, and, darn it, I was.

The sun set very quickly out in the desert but the exit did come complete with a stunning light show which I was lucky enough to catch in the rear-view mirror. The sky turned the deepest purple while a mass of stars gradually brightened until there was a shimmering canopy stretched over my head. It was the kind of night which made you wonder, is there a God? Why are we all here? And what's that strange ticking noise from the left-hand cam shaft? I pondered for a few moments then lowered my eyes to look across the dark expanse of desert where I could make out a pulsating multi-coloured band of lights floating in the air miles ahead of me. Either some strange force of nature had dropped Blackpool in the middle of the desert (unlikely), or I was approaching the Nevada state line. Realisation dawned fast that I had arrived in a state unlike any other in America, where gambling is more than just legal, it is well nigh compulsory. Two inches into Nevadan territory, precisely in the middle of nowhere, they had taken hideous advantage of the state laws to build two large casinos which looked like the tackier sets from *The Prisoner*. I managed somehow to avoid the bouncing ball as I stopped to take on burgers and gas. I was saving myself and my money for the real thing and now there were only fifty miles to Vegas.

Chapter Two

Las Vegas, Nevada
and Salt Lake City, Utah

I'd never been to Las Vegas before and the strangest thing about arriving there was that it all seemed so familiar. *Déja vu* and neon. As I drove down the Strip I was greeted by a string of old friends from movies: the Dunes, the Sands, the pure campery of Caesar's Palace, the Flamingo, all introduced by those huge signs with the names of the superstars on stage. How very different, I mused, from our own dear Largs.

Now to find the hotel. It would be difficult to miss, being the biggest in the world (if you discount the 5,000-room Hotel Rossiya in Moscow, which, strangely, in Las Vegas they did) and being the only hotel in town with a full-size Arthurian castle made of brightly coloured Lego in the centre of it. I have to say that an open-top '51 Cadillac was the only way to arrive in this town. You would, for example, feel a bit of an arsehole cruising the flickering streets in a Fiesta. Excalibur, for so my destination was called, lay at the southern end of the Vegas Strip and was so outrageous in its design that it made the rest of this tacky town

look like Vienna. I drove the Cadillac into a massive reception area where I was attended to by a young varlet called Hutch dressed in traditional yellow polyester pantaloons above historically correct Nikes. He looked like a drunk's description of a Swiss Guard. The walk into the hotel was a complete sensory experience. I was assaulted by garish colour, a cacophony of jangling bells, clattering money and nervous chatter, the smell of cheap perfume and electric motors, and the tingle of static from too many man-made fibres as every kind of gambling known to man went on around me. It was like that at 2 am when I arrived and exactly the same at 7 am when I got up to start filming (yes, showbiz is hell).

The only way to get to your room from the front desk was to cross the massive casino floor, which meant that it took most people two hours and a week's wages to get there. Hutch guided me expertly through the maze of 3,000 slot machines, pausing only to allow me time to attempt to lose all the contents of my pockets on the way (I actually won forty dollars from one machine. Gambling is easy, I thought). And, boy, did I need a tracker to read the spoor on the swirling Axminster, as there were no signs to help you get anywhere. Entirely deliberate policy by the management, of course, because a man who gets too speedily from A to B might just miss a blackjack table. I was surprised to see there was no craps game in the elevator but neither was there a remote control on the TV in my room. After all, Johnny Lie-a-bed, scratching his bahonkas, cannot possibly be downstairs feeding those slot machines until his thumbs are a blur, can he? Did I describe the room? Let's just say that when Tony Curtis shouted, "Hey, my liege, let's go to yonner castle," this was the castle he had in mind. It was as yonner as they get.

There are over 4,000 rooms in Excalibur, all based on a Vegas designer's idea of what Camelot was like (and here I suspect the employment of hallucinogens). I leave you to imagine the results, although a clue to the scale of the place is that the cabaret at dinner every night involved six Knights of the Round Table and their horses having a full-scale jousting tournament while the Chicken à la Elvis was being served. A sign on the wall of my room said the room rate was $200 a night but actually everyone gets in for forty dollars because the management need you and your quarters there in the certainty that the two of you will soon part company. The theory seems to work because twenty-two million people come to Vegas every year and leave behind a staggering ten billion dollars when they go. Only ten per cent of those visitors get out of town with a profit, which meant I was currently in the top bracket. Statistics suggested that I would not stay that way.

Las Vegas exists for one reason only, and that is making money. Gambling was legalised in Nevada in 1931 but it took the influence in the Forties of a lot of chaps whose names rhymed with ravioli to create the multi-million-dollar leisure complex of today. During the Thirties Vegas had been just a dusty stop-off point on the railroad for soldiers on their way to California, with some small-time gambling and prostitution. Then along came Bugsy Siegel, the handsome Murder Inc. operative, who had been sent to California to develop Mob interests. He was persuaded by his boss Meyer Lansky to look at the potential of turning Vegas into a money-making venture and raised six million dollars to build the first resort hotel. Thus was born the Strip. He called his luxurious gambling palace the Flamingo, but it failed to take off after opening in 1946 and Siegel's investors extracted a high price for the lack of return. Ironically, the Flamingo went into profit just months after he was found with five bullets to his head in his lover Virginia Hill's Beverly Hills mansion. The Mob influence has now been wiped from Las Vegas after a purge in the Sixties and shady investment has been replaced by good clean Corporation money. (Yeah, sure...)

The dream of every sucker (moi) who comes into this town is to find a system to beat the odds, or even, in my case, to find out what the odds are. I'd been told that the man to speak to was Howard Schwartz, a fast-talking Brooklyn-born guy in a baseball cap, who was a director of the world's biggest bookshop devoted to gambling. He told me the depressing truth: that even with the most intelligent system the fly in the ointment is not mathematical but emotional. Howard said the only successful method was knowing when to quit, and he had the figures to prove it. In card games you're at a four to six per cent disadvantage if you're not a good counter while a truly brilliant player can only give himself a two per cent advantage.

Games of chance like craps (forgive me, missis) are not so much about skill as being on a lucky roll. A hot roll can be spectacular and Howard told me about a guy of eighty-two who arrived with a social security cheque of $300, "ran it up to half a million dollars in two nights, but pissed it away at the tables the next night because he was a craps degenerate." Must remember that as a new insult.

Howard also knew about many of the elaborate scientific and technological attempts to break the bank. There were the Physics professors who invented a mini-computer which calculated if a roulette wheel was even microscopically off-centre and gave them a highly lucrative forty-four per cent advantage as they played. The device had to be kept in the players' trousers but tended to overheat and emit clouds of smoke – always a dead giveaway, I find. Nowadays all the tables and games are electronically "swept" for devices in case of less obtrusive devices. Howard seemed to know everything there was to know about gambling but confessed he was not much of a dabbler himself. As he put it, getting involved for him would be like "a diabetic being let loose in a candy store." He was staying sugar-free and sane.

As I looked around the packed casinos and hotels I realised that Las Vegas, despite its shady past (and possibly present), has an air of innocence which makes the place like a grown-up's Disneyland. Middle-aged America flocks here in their thousands and everywhere I looked there were mature couples walking hand in hand and snogging in doorways; and it was obvious they were all married. To each other. Really. The truth about the place is that the average punter comes to Las Vegas for three days, spends three hundred bucks and has a lot of fun. People say that they have lost that money but I disagree. After all, when you've had a nice Ruby Murray you don't say you've lost fifteen quid, do you? Vegas was a place where you could have a guaranteed good time, as long as you were not thinking of becoming a craps degenerate.

I stayed a day and two nights in Las Vegas and, yes, I did clean up. I would be happy to reveal my system, and will do once I have worked out what it was. In the meantime, how to spend all those winnings? I'd already invested in an Elvis bottle-opener, a tube of Wayne Newton toupee adhesive, and a Patsy Cline handkerchief, so the crew's farewell gifts were sorted out. What the hell, I'd just hang on to the other six quarters for the toll bridges.

I was on the road again and bound for a place I had always wanted to experience, Salt Lake City, Utah. It was Friday, October 23rd and I was driving north-east on Interstate 15 looking for the Great Basin Highway turn-off, thirty miles out of town. Behind me presidential candidate Bill Clinton was just arriving in Vegas (doubtless looking for my support), and above me four US Air Force fighters were staging a mock attack over the mountains to the north. It was as if Las Vegas had never happened, as the desert took over and I was on the straightest road I have ever seen, running for miles across a huge plain which shimmered like mercury. Modern cars are designed for effortless travel in country like this, with cruise control, positive steering, and air-conditioning, but those luxuries are for nancy boys who'd rather play a video game than drive a real car. Forty-year-old cars, even Cadillacs, have to be driven every inch of the highway and that suited me just fine.

Driving in the desert was a weird experience, surrounded by nothing

for miles except heat, dust and Joshua trees. It was hard to believe that anything could live here until you stopped for a slash and saw a huge snake crawling around in the dust (steady...). There were also road runners and rabbits living in what seemed to be no more than sand. It made you realise that the Life Force is pretty irresistible. A few straggling cattle in the distance reminded me of the pioneers who had dragged their unsprung carts across this hostile landscape. And what tough buggers they must have been, struggling a few miles each day lugging babies and belongings, constantly worrying if the food would last, and where the next water would come from. It was making me feel a pampered softie in my twentieth-century comfort when the Cadillac engine started rocking about Elvis-style on the chassis. I knew immediately that it was what Ed had predicted, an oil-soaked engine mounting, and I would need some help very soon.

The highway ran close to the old Santa Fe railroad as I made my way, more carefully now, through the desert. The Santa Fe boasted some of the finest railway architecture in the States: a strange blend of Hispanic and Edwardian which has always charmed the pants off me. So much so that Edward Hopper's painting of a Santa Fe railroad signal box was the model for the office atop my house. The railroad was financed by the Bank of Scotland (rather like several people I know) and built by mainly Chinese labour. It pushed West around the turn of the century, finally linking up this inhospitable country to the rest of America.

The long shadows of evening shone pink on the rail tracks as I arrived in a town called Caliente. The first sight was a huge Spanish-style station almost as big as the town itself: once filled with the noise of hundreds of miners and prospectors who flocked into town to make their fortunes, now only the occasional freight train disturbed the peace as it rumbled, wailing mournfully, through the old station without stopping. Nobody got off at Caliente these days and there was a sad, forgotten feeling about the place as I looked for a garage to tend to the ailing Cadillac. There was a choice: Caliente Autocare, or forget it. The garage came straight out of a Wim Wenders movie and the mechanics

had the facial mobility of Mount Rushmore. Dave and John fitted the new engine mounts Ed Sholokian had thrown in the trunk (bless him), but when the car was started a stream of sparks and a hideous scraping noise revealed that the new mountings were an inch short. The guys got quite emotional at that point and I swear I saw one of them change his expression for a brief second, but it may have been a trick of the light. There was also work to do on the electrical problems Ed had predicted to me a lifetime ago: the starter motor was being difficult, the regulator was wired up wrong and the dynamo was considerably less than dynamic.

The desert sky began to darken as we worked silently on. Sometimes I would leave the workshop where the Cadillac sat bathed in harsh fluorescent light to walk over to the railroad tracks and watch as the Union Pacific freight trains thundered by, all eight horns blaring. Trains make me feel good in a sad kind of way. What was it Scott Fitzgerald said about the mournful wail of parting that great ships make? The sight and sound of four yellow locomotives trailing fifty or sixty wagons through a Western town distracted me a little from the problems of the car.

At 9 pm the guys indicated they had done what they could and I was on my way again. I eventually made it to Utah in the small hours. In fact, rather smaller than I thought because on the way I had crossed from Pacific Time into Mountain Time and lost an hour. How I laughed!

Salt Lake City is an extraordinary place set in an even more extra-ordinary landscape. Backed by tall mountains, it lies on the edge of what was once a huge inland sea which stretched into Idaho and Nevada but has now mainly evaporated to leave the second saltiest body of water in the world surrounded by acres of salt flats. This is not the kind of salt you would put on your chips and is actually quite whiffy, which explains why the flats are mainly just a playground for the US Military and a select band of wild and crazy racers who attempt to break Land Speed records at Bonneville. Watching the clean white light shimmying off the salt, I couldn't help thinking about the great

Donald Campbell blasting along here at 350 miles an hour in Bluebird. Now guys use rocket power to do nearly double that, silly boys that they are. During Speed Week in August anyone who wants to can bring the family Buick Skylark to try to lose half a second off the standing quarter mile. Some people have been doing that with the same car since about 1962, God bless 'em.

I wanted to come to Salt Lake City to find out more about the Mormons (honestly). I'm not particularly religious myself but am fascinated by the intensity of the American approach to worship. The Mormons, or Latter Day Saints as they prefer to be called, came to Utah in 1847, having been asked to leave everywhere else (I think I now know why) and currently make up seventy per cent of the population of the state, so their influence is all-pervading. The city looked as though it had been scrubbed clean and had streets which were almost unreasonably wide. The sidewalks were deserted as I arrived at my motel which turned out to be a bit too close for comfort to Temple Square, the historic centre of the Church. It was Saturday night but it might have been Sunday morning for all the sparks that were flying. The State of Utah may share a border with Nevada but that is all they have in common. Taking a refreshment, which I like to do occasionally, is not illegal in Utah, but who could tell? Can you believe it is against the law for waiters to offer you the wine list because that could be interpreted as an incitement to take alcohol? "Waiter, I find I have quite spontaneously decided to have a drink, in moderation, of course. Do you happen to have a wine list secreted about your person?"

Next morning was grey and damp as I walked through the west gates of Temple Square looking at the Mormon Temple in front of me, a rather industrial-looking granite building with a bright gold statue on top. All that granite plus the weather reminded me of Aberdeen, but there the granite seems warmer and it is a lot easier to get a drink. I was on my way to the famous Mormon Tabernacle to watch the 3,297th transmission of *Music and the Spoken Word*, a sort of *Highway* for Mormons. The build-up had been tremendous: you were proudly informed that this was the longest-running programme in broadcast history and it was obvious the Tabernacle Choir had an almost mystical status in Mormon circles. The show was hosted by Lloyd Newell with the sort of voice that sells retirement condominiums on the radio, and featured a lecture on Family Values (my favourite), a guest appearance by the Air Combat Command Heartland of America Band (wild) and the great Tabernacle Choir (sounding like the Mike Sammes Singers), but no overt Mormon message. The tape was offered round the world at no charge and, surprise, surprise, was taken by 1,500 television stations. It started to become clear how clever the Mormons are at selling their faith and why it is the fastest-growing religion in the world.

Outside the Tabernacle I met another weapon in the Mormon armoury.

Sister Burton was a twenty-two-year-old Californian blonde with a big smile, a long frock, and a mission to convert the world. She had put her studies on hold for eighteen months to serve the Church as a guide in Temple Square and was highly trained to deflect any difficult questions from me in between churning out her Tourspeak.

Okay, here's the pitch. There were white people in America long before Columbus: tribes who had migrated from Jerusalem to the Americas 600 years before Christ was born and who Christ later visited after the Resurrection. The history of these people had been recorded on a set of gold plates which were lost until the Angel Moroni appeared to Joseph Smith in the 1820's and told him where to find them. He translated the plates into the *Book of Mormon* which was a companion piece to the *Bible*, giving a Western-Hemisphere account of God's dealings with men. The new prophet spread the word of his revelations and the religion was born. Unfortunately, many non-believers disliked Mormons and they were persecuted and gradually forced out of the eastern states. At that time, Joseph Smith was martyred. The Mormons had to struggle west to find a safe place to practise their religion and despite great hardships got to Utah in 1847. It was there that their new leader Brigham Young pointed to an empty plain and said, *"This is the place"*. The *"place"* became Salt Lake City and the Church has grown from a small band of hardy pioneers to a congregation of eight million across the world who believe in the importance of Family Values and material success.

Sounds cosy. But why, I wondered, had they been so unpopular out East in their early days? Could it be something to do with the fact that they refused to pay taxes, had their own army and practised polygamy (element of jealousy there, perhaps)? They are no more popular now with other Christian bodies, who claim the Mormon faith is not Christian at all. Furthermore, Latter Day Saints have a problem with Christianity, in that to go to Heaven both the teachings of Christ and the post-Smith vision of faith must have been accepted. This leaves anyone born pre-Joseph Smith on an unstoppable escalator to hell, which is why Salt

Lake City has the best Genealogical Record Centre in the world. Here, you can trace these limbo-floaters and baptise them in the Mormon faith posthumously (handy...). Another questionable area for me was that over the years Mormon articles of faith and attitude have been made more Politically Correct by the President of the Church, in conversation with God. And so it came to pass when the US Government refused to deal with the Mormons because of their practice of polygamy the Church President in 1890 could reveal that God had told him it was wrong and no Mormon should do it any more (some Mormons still pretend He never said that). And it also came to pass shortly after the Church was accused of racism that the Word came through that all members of God's family were welcome in the Church. There hasn't been a rush.

Sister Burton was a nice girl but I recognised in her eyes the slightly glazed look of someone who believes without question, like a Chelsea supporter. She had read the *Book of Mormon*, accepted it, and that was the end of the intellectual journey required, as far as she was concerned. She took me through the two Temple Square Visitor Centers, both filled with rather naive models and drawings of Mormon history, and proudly described the highlights: the paintings of the great Ancient Prophets, including that very late qualifier Joseph Smith; the baptismal font which was so massive you could even get me in it. "Oh Robbie," the good Sister exclaimed, "we could arrange that..." The climax of the tour was the chance to sit at the feet of a huge statue of Christ standing in front of a starry backdrop and listen to a tape of His word. Jesus, as far as the Mormons were concerned, had a voice like Pat Boone and lived in an early-Seventies disco.

There was not even the slightest chance of me wanting to become a Latter Day Saint, and Sister Burton, to her credit, was intuitive enough to spot that. She took her leave with the sound of Pat Boone echoing around us and I could not help but notice that the smile which had seemed so effortless and natural during our time together disappeared the second she turned to go. I would almost call her professional in her approach had she not told me that it was her own money funding her eighteen-month spell as a Missionary. Still, they gave her a nice badge with her name on it.

It was time to leave Temple Square and Salt Lake City and clear my head of all the clean-living conservatism I had been subjected to. Everything was so spotless it made me want to pick my nose and drop my trousers (that would have wiped the smile off Sister Burton's face. Or perhaps not...), and it was also hard to keep a civil tongue in my head in a state which makes abortion a capital crime. There are followers of every kind of religion in Utah but they are so much in the minority that they must have virtually no say in the way the state is run. Politically, it is quite common for elected representatives of the state to be non-Mormon, but to get elected and to stay that way any politician was going to have to heed most of the wishes of his predominantly Mormon electorate. I found it all quite disturbing and I couldn't help but think of the contrast between Salt Lake City and Las Vegas which was so marked it was hard to believe the two cities were on the same planet, let alone in the same country. This may have been the place for Brigham Young but it was certainly not the one for me. All I wanted was to get in the Cadillac and drive somewhere where people wore nylon shirts and sweated a lot.

Chapter Three

Southern Utah and Colorado

Utah has never been big on people and you can drive for hundreds of miles without catching a glimpse of a Utahan going about Utahan business, whatever that is. Those miles, however, were worth the driving because the state had some of the most spectacular scenery in North America and, probably, the world. Southern Utah, where I was headed, was the most stunning region with sweeping plains of Martian red dominated by surreal sandstone outcrops. If you've ever seen a car commercial then you know what Southern Utah looks like. Film people just love the weird locations down there and sometimes it is hard to move for crews queuing up to make movies and commercials. By a chilling coincidence there was a commercial being heavily played on American network television at that time which featured a black 1953 Cadillac Convertible driving through Southern Utah. It meant that instead of being seen as a man at the wheel of a powerful symbol of American industrial supremacy creating a fascinating counterpoint against the economically ravaged face of contemporary America, I faced the severe risk of being associated with a low-price burrito from Taco Bell. What made me feel saddest of all about the whole situation was that I don't even like burritos.

I left Salt Lake City on Monday, October 26th with a glad heart and a new starter motor which had required several precious hours of my time to fit that morning. Ed Sholokian, who had obviously kept his wings and halo hidden when I met him, was one of those people who symbolise the American attitude to service. Unlike other nationalities I could mention, if you ask an American for professional help it will be provided immediately, whatever time of the day or night it is. There is none of this "Mmm, I think we might be able to do something next Tuesday..." which we are all too familiar with closer to home. So when I discovered I needed a new starter motor, Ed was able to find one, put it in a plane and get it to me in Utah within hours. If only the quality of the fitting instructions had matched the speed of the service. I was lying under the Cadillac holding a very heavy starter motor in one hand and a sheet of paper in the other which in effect told me to:

a. Get starter motor
b. Fix it
c. Bugger off

I did manage all three instructions but it took quite a bit of skill, improvisation, knuckle flesh, and demented swearing. (Linguists will be interested to note that when Americans hurt themselves they use the same words as us. Like "Blast!" and "Naughty spanner!")

I headed towards Moab in South Eastern Utah, a small town on the Colorado River which had developed during the Uranium mining boom of the Fifties and was now at the heart of a second lucrative boom. This time people were flocking to Moab to seek out that precious material called Wilderness, and were prepared to pay through their collective noses to get as much of the stuff as they could. The town is perfectly sited for these outdoors men and women because it happens to be right in the middle of the most exciting theme park in North America. A park so wild not even Walt Disney could have created it, with miles of trails designed for state of the art mountain bikes and four-wheel drive jeeps, and with a stretch of water perfect for river-rafting, a sort of advanced fairground ride for jaded city dwellers which involves being strapped to a large rubber dinghy and screaming a lot. Moab was now full of places where you could buy or hire equipment to explore the wilderness and also full of places where you could stay in comfort if the wilderness got a bit wild for you. Personally, I didn't think the National Park was improved by the presence of sporty people with expensive running shoes talking vitamin slang or those folks on day-glo pink bikes with tight black shorts and half a boiled egg on their heads. What ever happened to the old Sturmey Archer Three-Speed, a sensible pair of brogues, and "Last up Ben Nevis is a jessie"?

The place was magical and after a good night's rest in a local inn I felt a strong need to get in touch with Nature. Thus it was a Coltrane very much in harmony with his environment who arrived in Arches Park not long after sunrise the next day. As I stopped at the ticket booth the silence of the place was broken by a muffled explosion and I looked up to see a cloud of red dust half-way up the mountainside. It was a rock fall although not a very big one. I could tell by the number of park rangers who suddenly appeared on the scene that this was not an everyday occurrence and even a small rock fall around here qualified as a major event. Once she had settled down after all the excitement, the lady at the booth told me that I really would have a "wilderness experience" on this day because we were the only film crew with a helicopter in the park. There would be no other pesky movie-makers around to disturb the peace we were about to disturb.

The reason Arches National Park appears in so many movies, commercials and videos is that it has to be one of the most impressive backdrops on Earth. The incredible geology of the place was created when two massive plates of rock slid on top of one another one day, giving birth to a landscape that could be from another planet. A lonely desert is punctuated by huge slabs of rock as big as skyscrapers which have been worn into surreal shapes by millions of years of erosion by tiny rivers and wind-borne sand. It was difficult to believe what you were seeing: enormous boulders hanging on rocks which seemed too fragile to hold them, while huge cliffs had been made into works of art by the incredible arches Nature had worked into the stone. The stone is made up of layers of varying durability which naturally wear at different rates. The result looks like massive chocolate cakes, the arches being made when the "filling" dissolves (recipe: page 19). The beauty was stark and I, for one, found it hard to put into words what connection there was between this awesome place and a low-price Taco Bell burrito.

It had been decided that I should follow in the tracks of *Indiana Jones* and *Thelma and Louise* by being filmed driving through the middle of the ultimate film location. I confess that I did have a few misgivings about the negative effect the helicopter would have on the natural balance of the area, but the park rangers were surprisingly quick to put my mind at rest. These National Parks are owned by the people of America and the administrators in their wisdom have decided to allow limited filming within them so that more people can enjoy their beauty. We had to pay a fee for the privilege plus the costs of the policewoman and sheriff who handled traffic control while we filmed our sequences, but it was all quite easy. I was amazed that America was so free with her resources, even to us aliens. The only problem of the shoot was having to face a lengthy and dull lecture from the Chief Ranger about the potential damage we could do to the environment during the shoot.

The truth was that even with a Bell Jet Ranger helicopter thundering away inches from my right ear I felt at one with Nature (yes, really) as I drove through the amazing spectacle of the park. The whole atmosphere was prehistoric and I just wished I'd been there the night those plates collided to produce all of this.

I left Utah without having felt the slightest desire to mount a mountain bike or straddle a raft, but I was definitely in the minority. There is nothing Americans are more serious about than fun, and around Moab there were many grimly determined people carrying and wearing lots of expensive gear with the intention of having a good time, even if it killed them (it does, sometimes). The mountains were all theirs, as far as I was concerned, and so, come to mention it, were the other so-called highspots down in town. I had been pleased to see there was little sign of Mormon influence out in the wilds but in Moab the licensing laws still bore the mark of their fundamentalist style. I admit I was surprised to discover that it is actually illegal to drink wine in a bar but I now realise how important a law that is. People would start with just a sip, then before you know it they would be asking for whole glasses of the stuff and the slide down the slippery slope might have ended in, dare I say it, fun. Those Mormons certainly have their priorities in the right order.

I made a textbook escape from Utah, perfect except for one tiny detail: I got stopped by the police. I had headed north from Moab on Route 191 past the old Uranium mine (can't miss it, glows in the dark) and joined the eastbound Interstate 70 at Crescent Junction. From there it was just sixty miles to the Colorado border and normality. I gave the gas pedal a celebratory push and Utah disappeared behind me satisfyingly quickly. The border was almost in sight when I saw the flashing light in my mirror and realised that the Cadillac was doing a very comfortable, but not very legal, seventy or so miles per hour. A highway patrolman's nose had homed in on my speed a little earlier and was telling me to pull in. It looked like it was time to use the secret weapon I had been carrying since I arrived in America, a weapon so

powerful if used correctly it could stop a law enforcement officer dead in his tracks. Yes, it was time to use my Scottish accent.

It's a sad fact about America's rampant gun culture that stopping a motorist is now one of the most dangerous things a police officer can do. As the officer walks towards the car from the rear the driver tends to reach to the glove locker for his or her driving licence, a move which could equally be for a concealed gun. This fear meant that I was being approached by a policeman who had unfastened the clip on his holster and was dangling a gloved hand over the exposed revolver butt. A foreigner quickly learns not to call behaviour like this paranoia. Watching a bit of television in America will fix that. Viewers are now bored with fictional cop shows with their excess of fake violence, blood, and murder. They want real cop shows with real violence, blood, and murder, and television producers with access to police and witness videotapes of real crimes are satisfying their need. The networks are now filled with shows based on "actual tape" of horrible crimes or graphic reconstructions of incidents which are often introduced by the poor police officers who were caught up in them. The message from these shows is clear to anyone on the streets of America: make a wrong move and you are very dead, very fast. I sat absolutely rigid in my seat as the policeman walked slowly up to the car window.

The sun caught the cop's shades as he leant towards me but I still got no clue about what was going on behind the heavily tinted glass. His mouth told me that he wasn't smiling and as he began to speak it did cross my mind that he might be about to arrest me for use of a controlled substance (a glass of Chablis in that bar in Moab). In fact, he had just clocked the Cadillac at 75 miles an hour, which is 10 mph above the limit for Interstate driving. I hit him with some Caledonian charm but my tartan twang fell on deaf ears. He asked for my licence, called it in to his headquarters and waited for the word. The bike radio crackled back the news that because I was an alien they could not press charges for my traffic violation and so I was free to go, as long as I did that going at no more than 65 mph. Heady with the sweet taste of freedom, I felt confident enough to tell the officer how much of a disappointment he was to me. To be stopped by an American cop on a motorbike was to play a part in a classic American scene, for Chrissakes, but the illusion had been shattered when I discovered the bike he was riding was, horror of horrors, Japanese. If an alien like me had enough belief in an automotive icon to cross the whole of America in a Cadillac why could the Utah Police not patrol their beat on Harley Davidsons, Lord help us? Had the Boys in Blue no soul? I got the impression that the man on the Kawasaki was not in the mood to discuss the subject. He muttered something I didn't catch (something to do with Fat Jocks) then climbed aboard his two-wheeled treason machine and I watched him whine (definitely not roar) off into the distance.

A week into my Grand Tour and I had already decided which state of the Union was my least favourite. I was glad to see the back of Utah, spectacular as much of it was, and I could feel a weight lifting from my shoulders as I crossed into Colorado. The trees that lined the banks of the Colorado River which ran alongside the Interstate still showed Fall colours but the weather was beginning to deteriorate. It had got much cooler as I drove through Utah and now the roof of the Cadillac was up for the duration. The forecast was for snow as I crossed the Rockies and all I could do was hope that the forty-year-old heater at my feet was working better than the other dodgy Cadillac electrics had done so far. I followed route 70 east through Grand Junction and Glenwood Springs before striking out into the mountains at Vail, one of those Colorado ski resorts where steamed-up goggles hide some of the most famous faces in the world. I was on Route 24 south through the Rockies on a switchback ride up and down 10,000-foot peaks, with snow beginning to challenge the power of the Cadillac windscreen wipers. The heater was also fighting a losing battle, even with a huge lump of cardboard covering the radiator.

The date was Thursday, October 29th and America was five days away from a Presidential election. Bill Clinton was leading the polls by a mile and from the sound of things the American right wing was

panicking. The spokesman (self-appointed) for that section of the population was a radio broadcaster with the kind of name you only get in America: Rush Limbaugh, whose daily morning talk show was the hottest thing on the air in 1992. Limbaugh handled topics and callers with an articulate and often witty kind of bigotry which amused many Americans but also pandered to the extreme views of some of his compatriots. Broadcasting from what he called "The Institute for Advanced Conservative Studies" (or as I prefer it, the Bunker) Limbaugh poured scorn on the Democrats, anyone vaguely liberal, and particularly a group he referred to as "Feminazis". The show I was listening to had a surprise guest when none other than the Voice of Reason, Colonel Oliver North, called in with his thoughts on the Campaign. He believed that the polls were unfair because they were taken when all good Republicans were out at work and so gave a totally unbalanced picture of the electorate (I know, I know...). Life was too short to subject myself to the political opinions of Colonel North so I switched to a country station to make myself feel really bad.

I stopped for the night in a town called Salida which was surrounded by snow-covered mountains and the kind of ranching land advertising copywriters call Marlboro Country. In fact, the photographs for the campaign were taken at a ranch just outside town and I was impressed to see real cowboys around who looked like they had stepped out of the ads. Everyone was mighty polite in this part of the world and the country looked superb, so it was hard for me to saddle up and head out of town the next day without having the chance to rope me some steer, or indeed, steer me some rope. *Tempus fugit*, even in Colorado, and I had to get on the road again.

Chapter Four

Kansas

When this Cadillac was built back in 1951 America was at the peak of its powers. While Europe struggled back from the debilitating horror of war the Yanks were enjoying prosperity and a flowering of their own style, enshrined for me in the brilliantly confident design of the car I was now driving. It must have been a great time to be an American and many people I met on my trip, prompted by the sight of the Cadillac, hankered after those lost days of supremacy. But there is another time in the history of America which, despite being harder, poorer, and more dangerous, holds a much more powerful fascination for Americans and foreigners like me. Show me the man who hasn't felt a secret desire to put on a stetson hat, saddle up a Palomino, spit a thin jet of tobacco juice into the dirt, then form a posse to catch the bad guys, and I'll show you a liar. America's strongest and most enduring image is the Cowboy of the Wild West and I was on my way to the definitive Cowboy town, Dodge City, Kansas.

Compared to West Colorado, the Eastern section of the state was, how can I put it, scenically challenged. On one side you have the Alps and on the other you have East Anglia, and the change happens very quickly. Whatever your feelings about featureless landscapes, you are about to be part of one for many hundreds of miles. All you can do is hope the radio has got some interesting stations on it and try to stay awake. I had reached the Great Plains of the Mid West, traditionally seen as the dullest, most reactionary part of the country, where big news is a change in the price of grain and big fun is talking about it. There didn't seem to be much else to talk about other than grain because all I could see ahead of me was an infinite field with just the occasional farmhouse to break the monotony. The huge farms were sporadically enlivened by massive grain elevators rising from the flat earth like stranded ocean liners. They were often painted in alarming colours which turned them from being surprising to being plain unwelcome. It was nearly November but there still seemed to be plenty of activity on the farms with huge expanses of winter wheat (developed in Russia) swaying in the cold wind. The original farmers in Kansas were Russian Mennonites who brought their skills to these dry plains in the nineteenth century and helped turn them into the bread basket of the world. It has never been easy for the Kansans but even the farmers must find it hard to complain about land which lies over a huge underground lake to provide irrigation, beneath which is a massive oil field to help the bank balance. I started to notice small oil pumps dotted every few hundred yards in the fields, swinging rhythmically in a profitable dance. Ingeniously, many of the pumps are driven by tiny gas engines which run off the vapour coming off the oil well. Don't need any electric cables, the clever devils. Meanwhile on the radio the choice seemed to be between God and the Fatstock Prices. Welcome to Kansas.

As I pulled into Dodge City it seemed hard to believe that just over a hundred years ago this was one of the most exciting and dangerous places on earth. They used to call it the "Wickedest Little City" in America but as I drove to the motel it looked about as debauched as

Croydon. It was certainly historically accurate that Dodge City was a "wicked" place but the most extraordinary thing about this centre of Wild West legend is how short a time the badness lasted. Dodge came into being in 1871 as a base for the Plains Buffalo hunters but it was only when the Texan cattle drovers started to bring their herds to town in 1875 that the fun began. Wyatt Earp and Bat Masterson were the legendary Deputy Sheriffs who tried to keep order in a town which by 1880 had a population of 1,000 and a generous selection of twenty saloons to drink, gamble and fight in. Just like in the movies, Dodge City men were men and many were affected by sudden lead poisoning which required a one-way visit to Boot Hill but, unlike the celluloid version, not usually after a quick-draw gunfight in the street. Killing was a lot less glamorous and often involved bullet holes in cowboys' backs. By 1883 the wildness was going out of this part of the West, highlighted by the fact businesses were required to close on Sunday, and in 1885 the death blows to a way of life were struck when liquor was banned

and the quarantine laws stopped the Texas cattle drives coming to town. So there were really only five shoot-em-up years in Dodge City but Hollywood and, to a certain extent, the City itself have cashed in very nicely, thank you.

I knew the facts but I still wanted to live the Western fantasy so the next day I went to the Front Street Museum in town which was built behind a re-creation of the main street in Dodge as it would have looked in the late 1870s. The shops and buildings on the street confirmed that life on the frontier was not without comforts. The railroad could

bring high-quality supplies into town and the cattle men and cowboys had a fair bit of cash to spend, so after a hard day's riding tall in the saddle they could enjoy fresh oysters and champagne. Sure beats beans. The museum combined a quite scholarly view of the town's history with a chance to enjoy the Western myth. Outside local volunteers acted out gunfights for the tourists with Front Street as a backdrop. It sounded a bit tacky but it was actually a great show with a script which gave everyone the excuse to blast away with their guns for fifteen minutes or so. The boys were obviously donating all their free time and two thirds of their hearing for the cause. The leader of the gunfighters was called Del and he genuinely believed that one day a Hollywood film producer would happen to be passing Front Street, see the show, like what Del did, and sign him up to go to Hollywood. There is an unquenchable spirit of hope in Americans for which the only word we have in Britain is "stupid".

The gunfight at the OK Museum got me thinking about an inescapable fact of American life in the 1990's: the US Constitution allows millions of people to have guns and many of those gun owners shoot their guns at other people. I read some statistics at breakfast which nearly made me choke on my hash browns: there are 66 million guns in America; in 1991, 24,000 people were killed by hand gun, of which nearly 13,000 were homicides. I found some comparative statistics for 1990 which put this terrible situation in perspective: that year there were 10,900 murders by gun in America. In Britain there were twenty-two. I liked America a lot but I had to question a society in which twelve children were killed by hand gun every day. I decided while I was in Dodge City to find out about the modern Kansas attitude to guns and I stopped at the first gun shop I saw. Bob's Pawn and Gun Shop was a mile outside Dodge with a sign proclaiming, "We lend money on anything that doesn't eat". Bo Hill, a petite and pretty Calamity Jane type who ran the place with her husband Jeff, turned out to be an articulate spokeswoman for the pro-gun lobby and estimated that around eighty per cent of Kansans were armed. All you needed to buy a hand gun was

to be twenty-one, have a Kansas driving licence, the sense to answer no to questions about drug abuse and mental health on a standard government form, and about three minutes to wait. Bo believed if you outlawed guns only the outlaws would have them and she began to sound more and more like a character from a movie as her argument developed. "It's a dog-eat-dog world in this country," she told me, "and I'd rather be in the jail than the obituary column." There was nothing I could say to convince her that guns were a frightening scourge on American society and that her country would be a better place without them. I left Bob's Pawn and Gun Shop realising that you can take the American out of the OK Corral, but you can't take the OK Corral out of the American.

People in this country love titles which end with the words "...capital of the world", a phrase which I often find translates to "...capital of America", but Dodge City could lay claim to a title that really was global. The town was without doubt the "Beef Capital of the World". The Texas cattle drovers started it all back in the 1870s and now Dodge was the centre of a massive industry which processed (no mention of death here) five million head of cattle a year. I wanted to find out why this area had become the last address for such a number of beasts so I rolled down the Cadillac window and followed the smell. It led me to a huge feed lot on the edge of town where 50,000 cattle were gathered for the last round up before being moved to one of the vast packing plants in the area. A friend of mine who worked in an abattoir (must be the French for processing) once told me that the beasts always know what is about to happen to them when they get there. The animals I could see in the pens of this feed lot all looked happy enough at the moment because they were having a great time. They spend around four months being fattened up with a delicious mix of corn, alfalfa, and molasses which helps them gain over three pounds a day. Just to make sure, they throw in a nice steroid cocktail as well. The final ingredient is now ominously causing major anxiety amongst food scientists. I kept

thinking what life would be like here for a vegetarian. I know I wouldn't recommend anyone to try to follow a meat-free menu on a journey through Kansas. Remember, some people here can get quite upset by anti-beef views, and eighty per cent of the State is armed... "Who ordered the Tofu Burger?" Click.

I left Dodge City on a bright, cold morning as the packing plants spewed columns of white smoke into the still air. Dodge was a peaceful place now, even for cows, compared to how it used to be, and its people were old-fashioned country folks. That is polite, hospitable, and extremely right wing in their views. It was Monday, November 2nd and one day before an election the pollsters were predicting as a walk-over for Bill Clinton, yet I had hardly met a declared Democrat during the 1,800 miles I had driven from Los Angeles. Howard Schwartz, the gambling expert in Vegas, had been a real dyed-in-the-wool Democrat but pretty much everyone else I'd met was behind George Bush. The national polls showed that Nevada was still undecided, Utah was solidly for Bush, Colorado was for Clinton, and Kansas was split down the middle between the two. The Coltrane poll was saying George Bush was going to hobble back into the White House, but somehow I felt that I had not yet met on my travels what could be called a completely representative cross-section of the American people.

I was actually on my way to meet a group of people who had absolutely no interest in the outcome of the Presidential Election despite being American citizens. I remembered seeing the film *Witness* with Harrison Ford, set in an Amish community, and I wanted to take the chance of finding out more about these deeply religious people who wear seventeenth-century clothes and still speak old German. (And did all the girls look like Kelly McGillis?) I did know that they lived an insular life, had no interest in politics, and made cinnamon rolls which a man would die for. 125 miles east of Dodge City was the town of Hutchison and just south of there was a large Amish community centred round the village of Yoder. The Amish are the descendants of deeply devout and even more deeply conservative European Protestants who were persecuted as heretics for their beliefs and fled originally to Pennsylvania. They believe that man must be separate from the rest of the world to attain eternal life and stand for a devoutly religious, agrarian existence based around the family and community. They respect the traditions of their forefathers by trying to maintain a seventeenth-century lifestyle in America and have spread west to twenty states. America is generous in allowing its citizens to choose the way they want to live, particularly if they are good at it and don't bother anyone (and are white, of course). The Amish with their quaint garb and horse-drawn buggies are a strange but successful example of that freedom of expression. The down-side of being in America is that everyone else has the right to be a tourist so the Amish have begun to suffer a different kind of persecution, torture by camcorder. It is genuinely painful for them because they consider any kind of photography the equivalent of a graven image so refuse to allow their photograph to be taken. Not the best news if you were heading into Amish country with a film crew and wanted to make the right impression.

I had arranged to meet a man who was well qualified to discuss the Amish, and I took the liberty of making the location the Yoder Café which happened to serve those fabulous cinnamon rolls. So it was with extremely sticky fingers that I shook hands with Maynard Knepp, a compact baseball-capped man in his thirties, who had been brought up in an Amish family but became one of the very few people ever to leave the community and make a new life. The Amish believe in adult baptism which Knepp had not undergone, so at least he could not be excommunicated and thus completely cut off from his family when he decided to leave. As it was, he still needed a great deal of help and counselling to break the bonds of his upbringing and survive out in the world. He had met and married a Mennonite girl and now looked as modern as any of the farmers I had met on my travels. He could still keep close to his parents and he invited me to go to his father's farm nearby.

Knepp harnessed an old horse called Mack to one of his father's

shiny black buggies and took me out along the quiet lanes of Yoder beside small farms with ancient Dutch barns. It was bright and crisp and the scenery meant we could easily have been trotting through Northern European farmland. Knepp was proud of the brave leap he had made and was keen to talk about his life. He spoke the slow, almost halting English of a man who had conversed in German for much of his youth but his words carried a modern American cynicism about the religion on which he had turned his back. He missed the Amish sense of community but not the dark side of their beliefs which seemed to him to centre round Satan rather than salvation. Even strictly following the Amish way does not guarantee eternal life, which makes the real hardships of their existence difficult to bear. On the positive side, the community is incredibly strong and self supporting and quick to provide financial and practical help. If a man's barn burns down it will be rebuilt immediately by his neighbours, and when Knepp's father had a heart attack the community raised nearly a hundred thousand dollars for his treatment. Not surprisingly, the American medical profession loves the sight of an Amish patient because they have the rare quality of paying their bills on time in cash. And they never sue for malpractice.

But hey, excuse me, the Amish could use state of the art medical treatment but they were not allowed to have electricity and phones in their houses. They could use tractors to farm with, but couldn't put air in the tractor tyres. In fact, the Yoder community was currently in the process of splitting in two over the question of allowing air in the tyres of tractors. They have to wear seventeenth-century clothes but as far as I know Nike Cross trainers were not worn in seventeenth-century Switzerland and many Amish wore them now. The Amish obviously spent much of their lives making decisions about what was acceptable to whatever their image of being "plain" is, and because each decision required unanimous backing the process took a lot of time and a lot of pain. I found this concept of deciding when time had stopped for them all a bit farcical but they seemed to lead a peaceful, productive life, so good luck to them.

The most interesting thing Knepp told me about the Amish lifestyle was about their attitude to adolescence which sounds remarkably advanced. A lot of young people I know would be asking to join the Amish if they heard about their treatment of teenagers. When Amish

kids get to sixteen they are quite simply allowed to sow their wild oats with the tacit approval of their parents. They are too young to be admitted to the Church so they are permitted to go wild in this limbo period and they drink, smoke, and "mess around" with each other as though their lives depend on it. Knepp proudly showed me an old buggy of his which he had used as a teenager. It had a stereo, beer cooler and, I swear this is true, a pair of pink fluffy dice. Dating for the Amish is no problem because any family with a girl who has reached sixteen has to leave a light burning at night and any boy who calls in can ask her out. The young people party for whole weekends at a time and at night two, maybe three, couples get into bed together. Knepp told me with a straight face that all they did was sleep and nothing happened (what's always impressed me about teenagers is their sense of control in those situations...). There was something about the way that Knepp told me the stories of his youth which made me feel like he was sweetening the memories. I bet it was much less fun than he was making out. There were positive things within the Amish lifestyle but I have to admit that I disliked a code which shut you out totally if you decided to leave it. I found it hard to see any love or kindness in such an attitude and just wished that they could all be big-hearted existentialists like me. Then the world would be lovely...

Kansas may have had a reputation for being boring but I was finding if I scratched the Mid-Western surface there was a lot of stuff going on underneath. My next job, coincidentally, involved going 645 feet beneath the surface of Kansas to look for a true Kansan icon. One movie more than any other is associated with this state and for many people the best-known resident of Kansas is a young lady called Dorothy. Which is why I was pleased to hear that the original master of *The Wizard of Oz* was actually kept in Kansas in the safety of a deep salt mine. The mine provides space below ground with a perfectly even temperature of sixty-five degrees and constant fifty to sixty per cent relative humidity – perfect for storing movies, documents, magnetic data, even Government secrets. The only way down to the storage area was by a rickety lift which plummeted down the equivalent of fifty-four storeys in a very short space of time and in total darkness. It seemed to me that qualified as good security.

Max Liby, the mine manager, kitted me out with a helmet, emergency breathing gear, and glasses, all of which were new enough to make me look like John Major doing a photocall in a mine (I don't suppose he does many of those now...). I was then fully equipped to make a journey to the centre of the earth. The lift stopped in a wide tunnel about fifteen feet high which led out to the salt face a mile and a quarter away in the darkness (my stomach arrived later). I got a lift in a small Chevvy which was perfectly normal except that the roof had been sliced off at bonnet height, and away we went down the tunnel. Ahead huge futuristic machines roared in and out of sight, looking in the glare of the headlights like enormous insects feeding off the salt walls. I realised that those machines, even the Chev I was in, were much too big to have come down the lift shaft and must have been completely disassembled at the top, taken down piece by piece like Radar's jeep and put together again at the bottom.

The air seemed quite fresh and surprisingly warm in this sci-fi nether world. I did not feel any sense of claustrophobia, which surprised me, but I don't think I would have liked to be eating my lunch box down here five days a week. Just off the main tunnel a huge steel door marked the entrance to the storage area. A giant dimly lit cavern had been filled with rows of anonymous shelves brimming with mysterious cardboard boxes. I found prints from all the big film studios mixed in with terrible television shows which (strangely) someone had decided should be kept. There was *Taxi Driver* in a box next to *The Fall Guy*. Sacrilege. I've never understood why studios kept garbage like *Days of Our Lives* and scrubbed *The Ernie Kovacs Show*. Are they crazy? I spotted *Peyton Place*, *Diary of Anne Frank*, *MASH*, and a host of Forties and Fifties bad movies. With some guilt I realised I had seen them all. And enjoyed them. It was almost like I had found the Kansas equivalent of the Holy Grail and I took the elevator back to the surface feeling a warm sense of pride and achievement. So, not yet half-way and I was already completely insane. Things were all going terribly well.

The next day was Tuesday, November 3rd, 1992. For 266 million Americans the day they would choose the man to lead them for the next four years, and for me the day my Cadillac cracked a piston in Hutchison. It looked like the car would be going nowhere in the next twelve hours or so, very much like George Bush's campaign, unless I could find a good mechanic quickly. Yet again good ol' American service came to my rescue and a local garage got the piston replaced and me on the road again in a matter of hours. I wanted to get to Matfield Green, eighty miles north-east of Hutchison in the Flint Hills, where there was a ranch I had read about and very much wanted to visit. It was America's (probably the world's) only Feminist All-Women Dude Ranch and I had been invited to spend Election night with the rancher. Her name was Jane Kroger and something told me that it wouldn't break her heart if George Bush was kicked out of the White House as he now looked certain to be. I had heard on the radio just that morning that Bush had been introduced at a final rally by Mr Nasty himself, Rush Limbaugh. For once, the rats were climbing onto the sinking ship.

I drove east on Route 50 to a small village of wooden houses called

Cassoday where I stopped to get a bite to eat at the unpredictably named Cassoday Café. The first snow of Winter had fallen that morning and the café looked like a scene from a Western. Two horses were tied to a post outside the white-painted wooden building and I could see faces moving behind the steamed-up windows. Just up the street I saw a tall stranger turn towards me. He was chewing on a cheroot and wore an old poncho as protection against the icy wind. His eyes narrowed as I came into his vision. Was it my imagination or was his hand moving towards the pearl-handled Colt 45 at his waist? Sometimes I wonder what they put in the awful stuff they call coffee in this country. Anyway, the café turned out to be a kind of working cowboy canteen and I got talking to some of the boys as I waited for stew which had probably been cooking for days on the old stove. I couldn't help but think of my image of the men who ride the range and, sadly, these cowboys were not the type to ride into town, whoop it up in the saloon, have a wild gunfight and then head for the hills. They were more Perrier than Redeye, and they even talked seriously about caring for cattle. I found it hard to come to terms with a hard-bitten cowboy, the mud of the range fresh on his boots, looking me straight in the eye and saying, "What families want now is a lower level of unsaturated fat." The only real sign of traditional machismo from these cholesterol-free cowboys was a bit of tittering when I told them I was on my way to an all-girl ranch.

I got to Matfield Green late in the afternoon and pulled into a large yard with a couple of farmhouses looking across at a traditional Dutch barn. I could see there was activity at the far end of the yard where someone was feeding some very noisy geese. Jane Kroger was a small, fit-looking middle-aged woman in jeans who immediately made me welcome and invited me out to help feed the cattle. Her family had farmed the land for four generations and she had a dream, crazy she thought at first, to run the ranch with women only. The local ranchers accepted her because of her roots but were horrified by her plans. Now they grudgingly accepted that the ranch worked despite the fact women did the work. Jane had a couple of permanent helpers but she had also set up an organisation called "Prairie Women" through which women come out to the ranch to get away from the pressures of their world and have the chance to be ranchers for the weekend. Jane told me proudly that women were much gentler with the animals and the handling techniques she taught them made the cattle less stressed. Women also were better with each other under pressure and I remembered

hearing about the all-girl Round the World Yacht Race crew who did not shout at each other and went faster than many male crews. The women who were on the ranch while I was there obviously enjoyed working together and had a much greater collective spirit than the dull bunch of Cassoday cowboys I had eaten with earlier in the day. I had come to Matfield Green with just a sneaking suspicion that a feminist ranch would be all orange boiler suits, serial-killer haircuts and that I would be as welcome as … well, as a man at a feminist ranch, but I could not have been more wrong. Everyone I met was happy, fulfilled, and apparently not horrified by the fact I was not a woman. Women obviously gained a great deal from being on the ranch and even the animals benefited too, although apparently no amount of kindness saved them from McDonald's.

Everyone sat down to a farmhouse dinner, rounded off with lashings of cheesecake, and prepared to watch the Election. The television coverage was strangely muted and much less frenetic than our Election-night extravaganza – not, for example, a whiff of swingometer. The American networks had been criticised during previous elections for giving projected results before the Western polls had closed which had the effect of discouraging people in the West, three hours later in their time zone, to vote. This time I noticed that Dan Rather, the grand old man of *CBS News*, spent two hours stressing rather painfully that nothing was decided even though my granny could have told you Clinton was home and dry. Old Ross Perot blew all that for Dan by announcing live that Clinton had won a good hour before CBS could safely declare it. Clinton had amassed enough Electoral College votes to be President by 10 pm Kansas time although he did not appear to accept congratulations for another hour. I had also been right in my prediction of Jane Kroger's politics. She was overjoyed Clinton was to be President and we both looked forward to his victory speech. When it came it was a little disappointing, lacking in the rhetorical power you would want from the most powerful man on earth. In fact, it was Vice President Al Gore who made the best speech, filled with passion and enthusiasm for the future. I went to bed that night filled with new hope and confidence about tomorrow. Tomorrow we had to look forward to a new America, a better America, an America which did not have Presidential Campaign commercials every five minutes.

Chapter Five

Missouri

I switched on the radio next morning as I drove east towards Kansas City. It soon became clear that last night was no dream and the airwaves did sound beautifully clear of the incessant selling of politicians. I never thought I would see the day when commercials for haemorrhoid ointment would cheer me up but that day had come. Anything was better than some Coloradan Senate candidate using techniques I remember from the primary school playground to get at his opponent. Or some chocolate-toned voice-over merchant reading a list of qualities which more accurately described Mother Teresa than the local Congressional candidate who had paid for the praise. I could safely resume my search for a radio station which I enjoyed listening to, a search which had so far proved fruitless in some of the, how can I say, less musically advantaged states. I had come to the conclusion that the heartland of America was locked in a cruel time warp which prevented access to any music, fashion, or culture beyond 1978. The insidious effect of non-stop MTV had been to condition a generation into believing watered-down heavy metal played by boys with well-conditioned long hair was the key musical form. Anyone who disagreed had the right to be a country music fan. Music radio reflected this lack of imagination so a trip round the dial no longer wove a sound tapestry which captured the rich diversity of each county and state; all it did was throw up the same Bon Jovi track being played by 100 different stations. Where was the classic sound of small town America radio?

Kansas City sits on the north-eastern corner of the state which provides its name. Just to confuse weary travellers like myself, the main part of the city is not in Kansas but in the neighbouring state of Missouri. I did not have time to stop but I wanted at least to take a look at a town which played such an important part in the history of jazz. During Prohibition a corrupt local administration allowed alcohol to be served in the jazz clubs (hoorah!) and many of the great names like Ellington, Basie and Parker played here at the start of their careers. Kansas City did not look like a wild bohemian place now and I drove out of it with scarce a backward glance. I checked a few personal statistics to pass the time while I cruised across Missouri on Interstate 70. I had been on the road for exactly two weeks and had driven around 2,050 miles, which was 150 miles past the half-way mark on my route. The Cadillac was going well but the driver was finding the weather conditions trying. Ed Sholokian had warned me about the electrical system and I had been paying the price for a dodgy wiring loom ever since. The six-volt battery and the poor wiring meant that the headlights were not as powerful as they were designed to be (and they were designed to be terrible) which was no fun out in the middle of nowhere, a place I spent a lot of my time driving these days. Worst of all, the windscreen wipers and automatic windows which were driven by an ingenious combination of electric and hydraulic power were having problems. I could handle anything in the Cadillac but I had to admit being blind in a rainstorm did seem to affect my overall driving capability. The weather was getting worse the further east I got and I knew I would

face trouble later because of these problems. Still ... *Per Ardua Ad Astra*, as we say round our house, although not very often.

The radio in the dashboard of the Cadillac spat the usual chunks of predictable sound as I turned through the AM waveband. I was getting towards the middle of Missouri, and suffering the scenery deprivation I was always prone to when I did a long drive on a featureless motorway. The only sight which had caught my attention was a hoarding a few miles back which stood out among the standard forest of fast-food and beer signs. It was a big sign which read "Real Men Don't Use Porn". That's all and there was no indication of who had put it up. Perhaps I had reached the buckle on the famous Bible Belt which stretches across mid-America. Suddenly I was dragged from my musing by a voice brought into the car by a casual spin of the radio dial. It was a voice which seemed to come from American radio's past and echoed with small-town values and Mom's apple pie. This was radio the way it used to be: warm, homely and not very professional. I wanted to track the voice down.

Old-fashioned radio stations are always difficult to hide, probably because they tend to have 200-foot red-and-white masts right next to them. I knew the station I was looking for was called KWRT AM and based in Boonville, just a few miles from where I was. I followed the signs for Boonville off the Interstate then looked for a transmitter. It was not hard to spot and after a few minutes I was parking beside a medium-sized bungalow, the only one on the street with ten-foot-high steel letters on the lawn. KWRT "Hometown Radio" was the home of the voice I had heard. I went inside to find its owner.

The station was tiny and had a vaguely Fifties wood-panelled look to it. Country music was playing through a tinny speaker outside the studio while a man with headphones, who for a moment I thought was an accountant, looked through a pile of records. I waved through the glass and he gestured me through into his communication nerve-centre. Ted Bliel was a twitchy, bespectacled man in his mid-forties, and it was his flat, monotone voice which had led me to the station. Ted, it turned out, had been a broadcaster at KWRT for twenty-one years in which time he had become by far the most famous person in the area. It was said he could run for any job in the county and win, if he chose

to. There was no doubt, Ted Bliel was Mr Boonville. Incredibly, he displayed the same lack of emotion in person as his voice had on the air but he was interested enough to request an interview with me on his daily talk show which was due to start in ten minutes. We both squeezed into the tiny studio which was curiously unfilled by hi-tech broadcasting equipment and after the 10 am news Ted gave me a grilling.

I have been interviewed by many different journalists and broadcasters over the years but never by anyone so devoid of response to my words. Ted had no sense of humour; in fact, no sense of anything. His interview style reminded me of the man who did the Speaking Clock, but without his sparkle. After half an hour Ted threw the interview open to the people of Boonville to see if they could do any better. As I listened to a lady caller bring her singing dog to the phone I decided the answer was they couldn't. The singing dog apparently barked in time and tune with whatever refrain his mistress performed and the caller felt a visitor from Bonnie Scotland should hear this duet. I didn't have the energy to tell Boonville about *That's Life* (who has?), and apparently the dog didn't have enough energy to give me a song. The *Ted Bliel Show* finished at 11 am and the radio audience could relax again after the pulsating excitement of the last hour. Personally, I needed to lie down in a darkened room.

As I drove away from KWRT I still was impressed by what the station stood for despite my experience at the hands of Ted Bliel. It was one of a dying breed of small AM stations providing a service for a small

community and going some way towards preserving the kind of local values which bigger radio stations ignore. The operation could not have been much of a money-making venture for owner Dick Billings but he had a commitment to the area and employed that rare commodity called sentiment in his business decision-making. At least KWRT respected its listeners enough to sound like it actually came from their part of the world. More power to their transmitter was what I said.

I had 140 miles to go before I reached St Louis, Missouri (frequently mispronounced as *St Louee* because certain songwriters seemed to prefer the French version of the name). The Interstate approached the city from the north then swung south to follow the Mississippi into Downtown. I could see the great symbol of the city, the Gateway Arch, gleaming dully in the light rain ahead of me. This 630-foot-high delicate sweep of stainless steel was built in the Sixties to symbolise St Louis' place as the Gateway to the West and it became an instant attraction. (After a while in town I did wonder what the hell they had looked at before the Arch.) It was possible to be hoisted up inside a spindly leg of the Arch to peer out of tiny windows at the top but I decided nothing would get me up in one of those and stayed happily on Missouri soil. What really fascinated me about St Louis was that there were two cities here, one rich and one poor, separated by the river. The Arch stood on the Missouri side of the Mississippi with the prosperous, cosmopolitan city of St Louis behind it, while directly across the river and just into the state of Illinois was an urban nightmare called East St Louis which could lay claim to a list of the most frightening social statistics I had ever seen: of a population of 40,000, ninety-eight per cent of whom are black, around seventy per cent are on Welfare; the city has the highest per capita murder rate in the US, and an infant mortality rate five times worse than the national figure. I found it hard to believe that anywhere could be as bad as those statistics suggested, particularly once I was sitting in a very comfortable St Louis riverside hotel less than half a mile from this supposed hell-hole. I decided to get help investigating the story.

I knew where to go. In America the word journalist is not a dirty one and the trade is respected in a way that seems a distant memory to a British person. Unlike the UK with its huge selection of national papers, America relies on an army of local papers to do the noble work of the press in a quiet, business-like way, free from the excesses I was used to. In St Louis the local paper was one of the best in the country. The *St Louis Post-Dispatch* was founded and guided by the distinguished Pulitzer family for three generations and has been described as "the most effective liberal newspaper in the United States". I gave them a call and within minutes was speaking to the Editor; access in America means that anyone, no matter how senior, is just a phone call away.

The newsroom of the *Post-Dispatch* was on the third floor of a squat Forties block on the edge of Downtown. I'm always disappointed when I visit newsrooms these days because new technology has ripped the romance out of them and this one was no different. There was just a faint clicking of computer keyboards and a polite hum of discussion stirring the intellectually charged silence as I walked to the Editor's office. Nobody asked loudly for the front page to be held and there was not a single green eyeshade in sight. Still, Lou Grant would have fitted right in. William Woo was the paper's Editor, a serious man with a slow, very precise way of speaking, and he was fascinated by the story of my journey so far. He admitted East St Louis was a terrible blight on the area and told me if I wanted to find out more to speak to his Chief Reporter for the place.

Roy Malone was the man with the worst reporting beat on the staff but he seemed quite cheerful about his lot. He admitted he had been allocated the area as a punishment for a dispute he had had with management a few years ago, but he could handle it. A good-natured

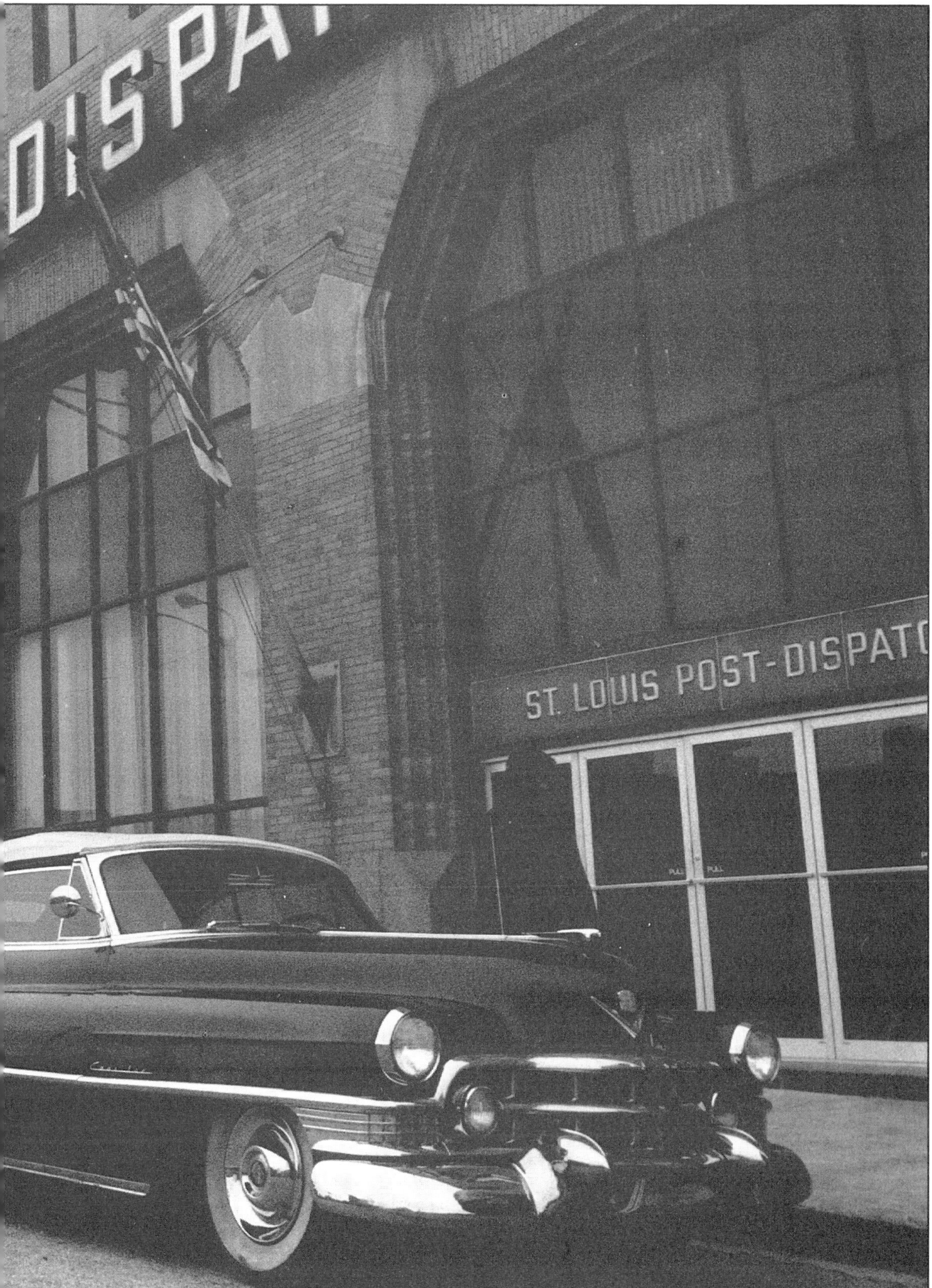
DISPAT
ST. LOUIS POST-DISPATC

guy whose face said "Irish", he had the obviously honourable intentions which make a person welcome anywhere. He was off to East St Louis to follow up a story he was writing and asked me along for the ride. I have to admit I felt more than a wee bit apprehensive about getting in his car and heading for the Badlands, but what the hell? Two Celts off to see the world. It had been done before.

We crossed the Mississippi on the Martin Luther King Memorial Bridge and left the comfort and safety of middle America for what was statistically an inner-city war zone. You did not have to be a social anthropologist to recognise the immediate signs of poverty in the streets of run-down houses with garbage strewn on their porches. As we drove Malone explained the origins of the urban disaster around us. While St Louis had always been rich and well-managed, across the river East St Louis had always been badly run by its City Hall and from the

late Fifties major industries like meatpacking, the stockyards and the
railroad moved out leaving few jobs and almost no industrial base. A
corrupt local government could do nothing to stem the flow and added
to the decline with gross mismanagement. The results would almost
have been funny, were it not for the human tragedy they caused. The
city ran out of money and had a police force that couldn't afford radios
which meant officers had to call for help from the nearest pay phone.
Not that the police were the lone guardians of order in a lawless world.
Malone told me the force was totally corrupt and that officers dedicated
their energies to avoiding crime, a suspicion confirmed by the statistic
that no policeman had ever been shot on duty. In a city with the
highest murder rate in the country. The truth was that being a policeman
was one of the few jobs on offer to the community. People were not
filled with a burning zeal to defeat evil-doers, they just wanted a pay

cheque so the East St Louis force had the best officers money could buy.

Pyramids of garbage covered every available space. Malone explained the mess was a hangover from the time when there was a "slight problem" about garbage collection. The city could not afford to pay for it for months and the rubbish was left to rot in the streets. Garbage was being collected again now, but they could not afford to clear up the mess of those lost months. I listened in amazement to a catalogue of total fiscal incompetence. The East St Louis Administration were so broke they decided to gamble on paying no insurance, got sued for $3.4 million by a man brain-damaged in a fight in a city jail, lost, and had no money to settle the lawsuit. The only thing City Hall had of value was City Hall itself. And so it was that the litigant woke up one day to find himself the owner of a very large Downtown building (only one previous owner). The Hall was returned to the original owners, eventually. In 1990 the financial position finally got so bad that the State of Illinois had to step in to take over the finances of the city, an act which Malone reckoned had given East St Louis its best bet for the future. Meanwhile, around me the dilapidated streets with burnt-out houses and blank-eyed men wandering aimlessly about confirmed everything Malone had told me. This was Capitalism's arsehole.

There was still some industry left in East St Louis but, typically, it was not the kind anyone wanted. Lurking just outside the city limits, and therefore not subject to any City regulations or taxes, were five chemical plants pouring pollution into the air of East St Louis. Malone drove me past one of the plants, a jumbled collection of aluminium towers connected by miles of piping and the usual hardware of cooling towers and storage tanks. What made this plant unique were the tiny houses scattered so close they seemed to be part of it – tiny wooden houses like Deep South sharecroppers' hovels which, not surprisingly, regularly fell foul of toxic spills from the factory. No-one had the political or economic muscle to defend the people who lived in them and there was more than a suggestion that the chemical company wanted the land they were on.

Malone drove on, talking positively about hopes for a regeneration which would only start if some jobs came to the city. He told me about some American Indians who were talking about building a casino in town which would bring employment. Ironic that the most abused section of American society, the Native Americans, could be the saviours of East St Louis. The city had also got a new mayor in 1991 who was attempting to clear up the twelve years of chaos under the previous incumbent and he had made improvements to the way the city was run. There was still corruption, however, because Malone was working on a story at that time about the whistle-blowing City Treasurer who had discovered one million dollars which had just been returned to the coffers from some litigation but had never appeared in the books. She was able to go public about the missing money because she was an elected official and could not be fired by her corrupt bosses. The flickering hope Malone talked about would always find it hard to stay alight in a place like East St Louis.

I slept badly in my comfortable hotel bed that night. I could hear the wailing of the police sirens from across the river as the East St Louis Police got to another incident much too late to save any lives. The only answer was new jobs, but which industrialist was going to take his factory into a society which could not guarantee law and order or a firmly controlled local administration? The circle was a vicious one and maybe impossible to break. As far as I remembered, none of the Presidential candidates had come to the streets of East St Louis in the last weeks. I supposed the positive backdrops and sound-bites required by the image-makers would not have been quite right there. The next day I would do what so many East St Louis people have done over the last forty years: get out of town, and never come back.

Chapter Six

Hannibal, Missouri and Fairmount, Indiana

I had avoided it from the start of this trip but eventually I had to do it for the first time after being on the road for nearly three weeks and 2,308 miles. I got into the Cadillac and drove west. It was not that I had decided to give up but simply because there was a place back in Missouri I very much wanted to visit. Hannibal is just a small town on the banks of the Mississippi but it is famous throughout the world as the home town of Mark Twain and the location for his most famous books, *The Adventures of Huckleberry Finn* and *The Adventures of Tom Sawyer*. I have always been a fan of Mark Twain's work and earlier in the year I'd had the chance to work in a new Walt Disney film called *Huck Finn* in Natchez, Mississippi with Jason Robards and Elijah Wood. Robards and I played a couple of conmen posing as Shakespearean actors and hit it off immediately as a double act. Samuel "Mark Twain" Clemens had been good to me so I figured I'd return the favour by visiting Hannibal. Twain was one of a handful of writers revered as a great American and I thought it would be interesting to see how his town paid tribute to its most famous son.

It was the kind of day the Scots invented the word "dreich" for as I drove out of St Louis. The top of the Arch was shrouded in cloud and cars had their lights on to beat the rain and mist swirling across the Interstate. The Cadillac windscreen wipers were showing their age with definite symptoms of senility in the cold, damp air. The electric windows had developed minds of their own. You'd press the down switch for back left and front right would immediately go up. It was hilarious, until the hailstones arrived. Then the air became full of words like "Darn those windows" and "I wish that electrician was here, I'd give him a bit of a talking to..." While I had been in St Louis the car had needed a visit to a muffler shop (translates into English as Kwik Fit) and another examination by an auto electrician. The upshot was she was as well as could be expected and only had to face 1,400 miles of evil winter driving before she could board ship for a nice gentle cruise across the Atlantic.

It felt strange going west but it was only thirty miles or so before I turned north on Route 61 which ran alongside the Mississippi River. This was Beef country but on a much more British scale than I had seen in Kansas. The small farms with their metal signs proclaiming the breed of their herds, usually Angus, looked just like home. I had noticed the Missouri beef producers were running an intensive, slightly aggressive campaign on the radio to promote eating beef. Rampant vegetarianism on the march in Missouri? I found that hard to believe, looking at the average menu, and come to mention it, the average Missourian. By the by, America is a most encouraging place to visit if you're on the large side (oh alright, a fat slob). I saw many people squeezed into shorts who made me feel positively anorexic.

I got into Hannibal around lunchtime and parked the Cadillac beside a restaurant advertised by a large glass of ale revolving atop a twenty-foot pole. I found the words on the glass strangely ominous. They read "The Mark Twain Dinette", and on the side of the building was the message "Home of Mark Twain's Fried Chicken". It appeared that when young Sam Clemens had lived here back in the 1840s he had had the foresight to set up a fast-food franchise operation. For research purposes I tried some of Mark Twain's Fried Chicken and came to the conclusion he made the right career choice. Not far from where I was eating, the river Mark Twain called "the majestic, the magnificent Mississippi" was almost completely obliterated from view by the dusty bulk of a twelve-storey windowless building. A giant grain elevator had been built right between the town and the river. Charming. My hopes were not aimed high as I set out to make a tour of the town Mark Twain used to call home. What would he, never a man to mince his words, call it now?

When in Hannibal, do as the Hanniballs do, so I wanted to travel in local style. I found a last vestige of the tourist season in the shape of a covered red cart attached to an aged but hyperactive horse and climbed aboard, prepared to see the worst. The driver was a tiny figure with a straw hat and a country accent. When he said his name was Glen Yoder it set off a few bells in my head. Yoder was not only the name of the town at the centre of the Amish community I had visited in Kansas but it was also a very common Amish surname. It turned out Mr Yoder did have an Amish background and I was to find out his story later. In the meantime, he encouraged his febrile horse to move and we plodded off through the streets of Hannibal. He told me in his opening remarks that Hannibal's only other claim to fame was a large cement plant which had been used in the construction of the Empire State Building and the Panama Canal, and it became plain why Twain was so important to the town. He was the difference between Hannibal being just another sleepy Hicksville or a lucrative tourist trap, and the locals had decided to cash in on his name in a serious way. Their attitude was pretty cynical. If it moves, sell it something; if it doesn't, paint "Mark Twain" on it. I saw the Mark Twain Hotel, the Mark Twain Wax Museum, Mark Twain Antiques, the Mark Twain Bookshop, the Mark Twain Riverboat, the Mark Twain Cave, the Mark Twain Supermarket and the Mark Twain Condom Dispenser (spot the deliberate mistake). Then there were the Twain characters' names, like Tom Sawyer's Snac Attac (sic),

TOM SAWYER'S FENCE
HERE STOOD THE BOARD
FENCE WHICH TOM SAWYER
PERSUADED HIS GANG TO
PAY HIM FOR THE PRIVILEGE
OF WHITEWASHING. TOM
SAT BY AND SAW THAT IT
WAS WELL DONE.

COLTRANE IN A CADILLAC

the Huck Finn Shopping Center, the Injun Joe Campground, the Becky
Thatcher Bookshop, and the name which surely would have Twain
birling in his grave, Tom and Huck's Go Karts. I thought I had read
Tom and Huck's adventures pretty closely but ... Mark Twain was a
man of acid wit and he would probably have laughed himself sick at
the whole shebang, but there was something kind of sad about it.

A sudden lurch from Yoder's cart yanked me back to where I was.
Strangely for a scenic tour we appeared to be in a narrow alleyway with
a view of a brick wall. The horse was munching on some grass and
Yoder had turned to look at me. There was something about his manner
which told me what was coming next. He was either going to get fresh,
or talk religion. Just my luck, it turned out to be the latter.

"This is not my only work." Yoder was gazing straight into my eyes,
and I noticed for the first time that he had a withered side. "Besides
doing this I'm a Baptist Preacher and what I am most interested in is
saving people. I was brought up in the Amish way but I was lucky, I
discovered the plan for Salvation. I learnt that Salvation is not something
you work for, as the Amish believe, it is something you claim by faith.
You must accept that you are a sinner and accept Jesus Christ as your
Saviour and you will have Salvation. Can I ask if you have accepted
Jesus Christ into your life?"

All I could think at that moment was that I had stumbled into a
re-run of *Wiseblood*. I also felt offended that Yoder believed he had the
right to inflict his views on me as a poor unsuspecting tourist. I suppose
I should have refused to discuss it any further but I couldn't help rising
to the bait. I asked if a mass murderer could get to heaven by accepting
this plan for Salvation. He gave me one of those non-answers which
left me none the wiser and we moved on to discussing his own story.
He had been happy in the Amish way until he met a man who taught
him how to be "saved". After that he left the community, taking his
now saved wife and five children with him, and began a new life. He
made his money doing the Hannibal tours for most of the year and also
ran a Baptist Church in a small town called Emden, Missouri. He spoke

114

sadly of the Amish obsession with living the correct life to get to heaven and how he realised that it meant nothing because none of them had been saved. Like Sister Burton back in Salt Lake City, Yoder finally realised he was casting his seed on extremely stony ground with me and decided to finish the Hannibal tour. I have no objection to people believing, but do I run into churches shouting, "You're wasting your time!"? No siree, Bob! So butt out, old buddy.

The final stop was at the bottom of a cobbled lane with early-nineteenth-century wooden houses on either side. This was the boyhood home of Mark Twain which had been completely restored in 1990, and nearby was Becky Thatcher's House, actually the home of Twain's childhood sweetheart Laura Hawkins. The most impressive house of the collection was the home of Twain's father J.M. Clemens who was Hannibal's Justice of the Peace. What they didn't make clear was the fact that the house had originally been sited in another part of town altogether and had been moved piece by piece to its new location. It was like moving Stonehenge to Trafalgar Square because it would be more convenient for the tourists. Another illustration of something I had discovered in my travels about the strange American attitude to their own history: what they prefer is a theme park version of the past in which historical locations are clean, accessible, and have all the necessary facilities. If a location fails on any of these requirements then the solution is to knock it down and rebuild it correctly. The American people are very proud of their heritage and they like it to be as modern as possible.

I felt very European and non-anally retentive as five litres of badness catapulted me out of Hannibal. My last image of the town was a view of Tom Sawyer's Cardiff Hill with the old lighthouse looking benevolently down on the mighty river. It was a fleeting but pleasing symbol of what Hannibal might have been, and the moment lasted until I remembered the lighthouse was a fake, built in 1935 to commemorate Mark Twain's centennial.

I now had some serious driving to do, beginning with a rather dodgy

metal bridge over the Mississippi into the State of Illinois for the second time on the trip. My first sortie into the state on my visit to East St Louis, had not done much to convince me to return but I gave it a second chance as I drove from one side to the other on the way to Indianapolis, over 300 miles away. I followed Route 36 to Springfield, then went on Interstate 72 to Decatur, joined the 74 at Champain, crossed the Indiana border at Danville and arrived in Indianapolis (pay attention, there may be questions later). And it was closed. The only famous thing in Indianapolis was closed, anyway. The Indianapolis Speedway, home of just one race a year called the Indianapolis 500, was undergoing renovation and I was not allowed to do what I had been planning for weeks, namely take the Cadillac out on one of motorsport's most hallowed tracks and burn some rubber. The people at the track told me that it wasn't safe because of construction vehicles. I'd like to have seen the JCB that could have got the better of Hot Wheels Coltrane on the banking. The Americans are very passionate, some might say precious, about Indy car racing, probably because it is another of those peculiarly American sports which calls itself a World championship but which almost without exception features American participants and locations. I contented myself with the knowledge, not quoted often here, that the most successful Indy car of recent years was actually designed and built in Kent. Makes you prahd to be British, dunnit?

It was Thursday, November 12th and the weather had turned very nasty. A massive cold front was sweeping the Mid West and appeared to be focused just above a '51 Cadillac which was driving north on Interstate 69 from Indianapolis, Indiana towards Detroit, Michigan. Gale-force winds buffeted the Caddy but it would have taken a hurricane to worry this two-and-a-half-ton beauty. Still, enough about me. The incessant rain had turned to a driving sleet, driving as well as I was, so I had great trouble making out the end of the bonnet, let alone the road in front. The Mojave Desert seemed a long way away.

I had one stop to make on the road to Detroit at the small Indiana

town of Fairmount, sixty-five miles north of Indianapolis. Fairmount was the childhood home of James Dean, the movie star who made just three films before dying in a car crash in September 1955 at the age of twenty-four. Too fast to live, too young to die. Fairmount was a classic American small town with a scattering of trim houses on tree-lined streets and a pleasant *It's A Wonderful Life* look. The Cadillac felt very much in place and in period as I drove slowly round the quiet streets. It did not take very long to see the whole of Fairmount and at first I couldn't believe what I had seen there. Or rather, not seen there. Not one single sign which featured the name of James Dean. No Dean's Dinette or Rebel Without a Cause Video Arcade in the home town of one of America's most enduring icons. This was a town which could teach Hannibal a thing or two.

Fairmount people are fond of quoting a statistic about their town which goes some way to explaining their low key attitude to James Dean. It had been calculated that Fairmount, with a population of a few thousand, had fourteen times the national average of persons listed in *Who's Who of America*. James Dean was the most famous but he could count as fellow citizens a list of celebs of varying magnitude: Jim Davis, the cartoonist who created a cat called Garfield (for which there is no punishment too severe); Phil Jones, a CBS News commentator; Robert C. Sheets, Director of the National US Hurricane Center; and Mary Jane Ward, a novelist. Fame was therefore a commonplace in Fairmount, and so a global teen icon was no big deal. Actually, the truth was that James Dean was a big deal who was almost more famous thirty-seven years after his death than he had been in his lifetime. His image had proved timeless and deeply attractive to both the disaffected youth of the world and to advertising executives – always a powerfully lucrative combination. Personally, I have never been a huge fan and for me he has always been a poor man's Brando. My critique of his acting has absolutely nothing to do with the fact that his picture is on every teenage girl's wall. Absolutely nothing. Honestly.

The Fairmount Historical Museum was the one place where the

COLTRANE IN A CADILLAC

town's memory of James Dean was on display. The museum was in a large red mansion house in the middle of the town and it was there I met a retired phone company worker called Bob Pulley who showed me round the exhibits. Pulley talked about Dean like they were old friends, which is exactly what they were. He and Jimmy, which is what he always called him, were classmates at Fairmount High and messed around as youngsters before Dean left town to try his hand at acting. Now Pulley was in his early sixties and had only recently decided to do some work with the museum, not to make money but just because he wanted to help the thousands of fans who visited the town and wrote to him from all over the world. He led me through a series of small rooms filled with glass cases which held memories of Dean's short but obviously happy life in Fairmount. He had a good upbringing with his aunt and uncle on a farm just outside town and was passionate about motorbikes, sport, drawing, and later acting. The museum was an intimate kind of place and as I looked at relics like Dean's train set and baby booties, I felt a real sadness, almost as if I was in the house of parents who'd lost a son and kept his room exactly as he had left it. Pulley had no answers for the questions I have always had about Dean, like how good he would have been if he had lived and why he had remained such an icon for young, especially European, girls. My theory is the Dean represents that magic time in most girls' lives, between ballet, ponies, and inept fumblings at bus shelters, when the vacuum must be filled by an idol who offers no sexual threat. Pulley did give me one fascinating fact about Dean. He told me that he stood one inch shorter than Dean and as he said it Bob Pulley pulled himself up to his full height: five feet five inches.

In keeping with the style of Fairmount, James Dean's grave was just another plot in the local cemetery. A sign at the entrance pointed the way to the site and it turned out to be a simple low headstone with a couple of bunches of fresh flowers and a pack of Marlboro Lights placed in front, and three or four recent lipstick marks around the name on the stone. All I could think was that it was probably the way James

Dean would have wanted it to be. The only time Fairmount lurches towards a kind of tackiness is every September around the anniversary of Dean's death when the museum organises a festival with showings of all his films, a Classic car show (no arguments there), and even a Dean lookalike contest. A tiny glimpse of the horrendous possibilities if Mr and Mrs Dean had been driving through Missouri when the baby James had chosen to be born.

I had spent longer than I had planned in Fairmount and was way behind schedule for the run to Detroit, Michigan. Outside the museum the sleet had turned to snow and I still had 260 miles to travel in a convertible car with visibility problems. It's hard when you come from a country where the sea is never further than ninety miles away to imagine the sheer scale of the States and its weather. The flat Mid-West landscape had no hills or valleys to stop weather roaring in from hundreds of miles away and that evening the storm was coming in like a train. I remembered poor old James Dean and reminded myself I'd have to be careful.

Chapter Seven

Detroit, Michigan

Life is cruel at times. In the movie in my head, the opening shot started fifty feet up looking across the windswept streets of Detroit. A newspaper would blow past, just slowly enough to see the headline "Clinton Landslide!" Perhaps there would be the traces of rain on the sidewalk, enough to reflect the crisp light of a winter's afternoon. As the camera craned down slowly, the road would fill more and more of the frame until the dark, satanic mills of Motor City lost focus and became a vague backdrop to a mysterious dark object roaring towards us. The camera would seem to duck under the road as the Cadillac, the sun glinting off its burnished chrome, came closer and closer still, finally flying over our point of view. In that brief second the car would effectively wipe the frame and in its aftermath we would focus on the massive letters on the darkest and most satanic mill of them all. The legend would be in sharp focus: GENERAL MOTORS. The car would have, literally, come home. Our hero would be seen enjoying (serenely, naturally) the whole symbolic importance of the car's return to the place of its birth as part of his overview of America Today. Fate, how-ever, had not been watching Orson Welles. Fate had been watching *Eldo*-bloody-*rado*. So I arrived in Detroit in the dark, nobody knew what they were doing, and there was nobody watching.

The journey from Fairmount had taken rather longer than planned. Something to do with the fact that I had to come via Antarctica. In fact, I've always said there is nothing more romantic than hammering through a snowstorm in a fine old motor. Even watching the drifting snow through the windscreen gives me that strange feeling of security you get sitting in front of a fire while the wind howls outside. But not when the snow is drifting *on* the windscreen, no siree, Bob! (Who was this Bob, I've often wondered, and what sort of a man was he to inspire the rest of us to greet him as "siree"?) As the conditions worsened I only had one windscreen wiper working. To be absolutely specific, there was only one windscreen wiper, the other having decided a life in the fast lane was too much for it and thrown itself under a Mack truck. The remaining solitary strip of chrome and rubber which was attempting to shift an inch of snow at each stroke was showing similarly suicidal tendencies, and was only being prevented from abandoning ship by the captain's beefy mitt. The Cadillac's interior temperature, which by this time was identical to the Michigan exterior temperature thanks to the window mechanism's warped sense of humour, was roughly minus fifteen. The historically accurate Cadillac crossply tyres, meanwhile, were making less than intimate contact with the icy tarmac. Is a picture developing here? Who the hell had got me, a rational person, into this appalling situation? And more to the point, who was going to get me out? I knew the answer because it was staring me in the face. The guy who was going to get a severe talking to was the guy wiping my windscreen. It was very late when I finally got to Detroit and I was not a happy bunny. The last hours had been hell and nothing this trip could throw at me from that time would hurt as much as they had. At least I could cling to that certainty, couldn't I?

The next morning I endured the most painful few hours I had

experienced for a long time. The date was Friday the 13th of November (and you know how superstitious we Luvvies can be); I had been invited to the Cathedral of General Motors to worship at the altar of Harley Earl. I was going to the end of the Cadillac rainbow to look at the riches there and, icing on the cake, I was going in my own beautiful Cadillac. This was to be a seminal moment in my life, and neither a miserable arrival nor a sleepless night on lemon yellow nylon sheets could ruin it. The Cadillac looked fine in the bright sunshine and biting cold of a Michigan morning and as I turned the ignition I could feel myself forgive her for the problems she had caused me. Two hours later I was sitting on the cramped bench seat of an official Cadillac flatbed truck, a comatose '51 Cadillac Convertible loaded on the back, as I turned in to the world-famous Clark Street headquarters of the Cadillac Division of General Motors.

The people at Cadillac, Al Haas and Greg Wallace, had been very understanding and got to my hotel as quickly as they could, but arriving at Cadillac on the back of a tow truck was like one of those nightmares which find you in the hardware department of John Lewis wearing nothing but a pair of someone else's socks. Blush City, Arizona. I had travelled 3,051 miles with the Cadillac wheel in my hands and for the only mile which really mattered, the 3,052nd down Clark Street, the only thing in my hands was my head. I felt angry and pissed off but in the midst of my self pity I found myself sparing a thought for the Cadillac. It must have been all a bit much for her coming back to her roots and the result was just a simple case of emotional overload. Keeping my own emotional overload in check, I prepared to step into Cadillac City, MI.

Cadillac was named after the French military commander who founded the city of Detroit in 1701, Antoine de La Mothe Cadillac. The company was started in 1902 by a genius called Henry M. Leland, a master of precision engineering and the pioneer of the standardisation of parts. He was a man who genuinely changed the world because standardisation was the key to assembly-line production and the shape of the modern

auto industry. Leland's company was bought by General Motors in 1909 and led the fledgling industry with innovations like electric ignition and the V8 engine. The Royal Automobile Club gave Cadillac the title "Standard of the World" in 1912 and the company lived up to that lofty badge for many years. It was not just under the hood where the Cadillac influence was felt and Harley Earl, the head of Cadillac's stylishly named Art and Color department, introduced the tailfin in 1948 which changed the profile of cars for two decades. Like all American manufacturers, Cadillac started to lose their way in the Seventies but nothing can ever tarnish the reputation of an auto legend amongst those who have been initiated and, believe me, I am that soldier (the ceremony involves four pistons and a lot of treacle and makes the Masons look like a bunch of silly wee boys in aprons).

Somewhere in the bowels of this enormous plant my Cadillac was being fussed over by a man in a blue coat as I took an elevator to the second floor of the building. Cadillacs are still built in Detroit but there is now a futuristic plant at Hamtramck which is highly productive but cannot compare in terms of romance to the place I was walking through. The floor was rubbed smooth and shiny by fifty years of car workers tramping to work and there was a definite sense of history about everything. I had somehow imagined that Cadillac would have been the kind of company which would have bucked the anti-history trend I had identified in the American character and kept a definitive collection of their work. In fact, Cadillac had never seen fit to keep examples of their cars in one location and it was only because members of staff had the enthusiasm and pride in their product to assemble the beginnings of a collection that I was able to step into a Detroit version of Sholokian's Cave. Cadillac had given the space for the museum but the workers had done the rest, and what a job they had done. Friday the 13th had turned out to be not such a bad day after all, luvvie.

The museum was in an old assembly area of the factory. Above my head I saw the tracks on the ceiling on which the machinery had flown into place, the line having been designed to be instantly converted from car to military production. It looked like a well-lit church hall but instead of maladjusted youths playing ping-pong there were lines of the most incredible Cadillacs. Ed's place had been impressive but this museum had some stunning cars. Like a wee boy taking the lid off a selection box, I took a deep breath and prepared to get busy. My eye was drawn first not to the sight of a sleek dream machine but to a chunk of raw power mounted on a stand.

The V8 engine, for forty years the heartbeat of American com- munication, was a solution to many of the early problems of the internal combustion engine. As you will know from your Newton, the accelerating mass (weight) of a piston, driven by the explosion of gasoline and air (combustion) is balanced by a similar force the other way. Although this force is absorbed, partly by the restrictions of the crankshaft via the connecting rod (if it wasn't the hills would be alive with the clank of flying pistons) and partly by the fact that an identical piston is shooting up on its compression stroke, this is happening several thousand times a minute and the result is that the engine, if left to its own devices, would bounce about like a drunk on a mattress. They tried lying the engine on its side, which only produced the same problems horizontally that had vexed them vertically (bored yet?). Putting the engine at a slant at least split the shoogle two ways, as it were, but the answer, to have two counter-slanted engines connected to one crankshaft, came in 1915. I just thought you should know that.

The sight of a piece of engineering brilliance got me thinking about the creative hotbed that Detroit had been. Cadillac, for example, introduced electric starting in 1912 (British cars were still offering heaters in cars as an optional extra in the late Fifties. We knew how to look after our motorists...) and these kinds of innovative design were as common as paintings of "Madonna and Child" in seventeenth-century Florence. The concentration of brilliant engineers and designers who had flocked to Detroit from all over the world would never be seen again. There were a dozen or so houses down by the river where, it is said by those who know, the dozen smartest engineers the world had ever seen lived

in a Florence of their own. Henry Ford in his wisdom, however, made sure that the force of innovation was quickly overpowered by the drive for standardisation and soon there was only Cadillac spending money on research. The battle was no longer to produce the perfect automobile, but the affordable one. So there you go.

The museum collection covered the whole ninety-year history of Cadillac and I saw fantastic examples from every decade, including two of my special favourites, a '56 Coupe and a '49 Sedanette. There were also one-off cars like an obvious precursor to the Batmobile, snappily called "The Experimental Laboratory on Wheels". Everywhere I looked there were sweet, sweet motors which reminded me of what I liked about Harley Earl's design: created to look like a dream, to let the imagination soar, to create an environment quite unlike anything the driver would see in any other area of life. I wandered happily through the serried ranks of perfection and then the good news came through that "She who must be repaired" was ready at the garage. It only took three security men to drag me weeping off the bonnet of a '33 Sports Phaeton, and I was off.

I decided to take a drive down Woodward, the avenue which carries a perfect straight line from the heart of Downtown through the middle of Detroit. It was more than an avenue, it was a living history lesson on the rise and fall of a city. Woodward started down at the rather scruffy area where America was separated from Canada by a narrow stretch of water spanned by the Ambassador suspension bridge and the Detroit-Windsor Tunnel, then headed north-west through a central area which had the usual glass and concrete towers of an American city but a noticeably different look. Detroit is a predominantly black city which made a huge contrast to the white heartland I had been crossing for weeks. Americans call this phenomenon of a wide ethnic shift "White Flight", and in Detroit it had been provoked by the city's race riots of 1967 which left over forty dead and were the worst in America's history until Los Angeles. The city is now seventy-five per cent black and the streets around Woodward showed that percentage clearly. As I drove, it was nine days since a black man called Malice Green had been hauled out of his car in town and beaten to death by police. A hysterical media had predicted a Los Angeles-type response to the incident but the people of Detroit had remained admirably calm.

I drove on and suddenly in the middle of the office blocks I saw the ornate front of the Fox Theater, the live mecca of great Motown acts in their heyday (wish I'd been around for that). Woodward started to look much more seedy around there but in between the adult movie theaters and the run-down shops were the cultural pearls left by the auto industry at its peak: the Orchestra Hall, then the Detroit Institute of the Arts, one of America's largest galleries. I began to see factories, now in decay, but at the time when my Cadillac was built in 1951 working at full capacity. It was an era when American industry ruled the world and General Motors was the biggest employer in the country, ahead of even the Army or the Post Office. The world changed but the complacency of the American auto industry meant it failed to notice and Woodward's boarded-up buildings and discount stores told the story of the result in Detroit. The figures were staggering. General Motors had laid off 70,000 workers the previous year and just that morning Chevrolet had announced they were laying off 11,000 middle-management employees. I decided to drive back to my hotel but as I was about to turn the car I noticed an incongruous plaque outside a derelict factory. I stopped and read that I was standing next to the Highland Park factory on Woodward which had been the home of Henry Ford's Model T assembly line. Detroit's history started here. But then history is bunk.

Ever since cars have been built the men who work on making them have inspired a strange kind of resentment because outsiders believe they earn huge sums of money for doing very little. I had read a terrific book which had taught me a lot about this deeply misunderstood breed. It was called *Rivethead* and had been written by a former GM Trucks Division assembly-line worker, name of Ben Hamper. It was one of those rare books you read and keep thinking, "Boy, I'd like to meet

this guy". And so I did, in his home town of Flint, fifty miles north of Detroit. Flint was the birthplace of General Motors and had been an auto town for decades. *Rivethead* was a blackly hilarious story of the ways Hamper and his fellow "shop rats" battled the mind-numbing boredom and danger of their work by bending the system as far as they could while still producing the goods. Hamper was seminal to understanding the sickness in the American auto industry since he had spent years at its Front Line. He was a small man with a dark moustache and as he talked the dry wit of his book came through. He took me first to the huge Chevrolet factory known locally as "Chevvy in the hole" where there was the sit-down strike in 1937 which gave difficult birth to the Union of Auto Workers. Hamper said that the loss of jobs was now so bad in Flint that maybe the time was coming for another strike. Every worker was scared that whole plants would be shut down and the work shipped to Mexico where the locals were paid twelve cents an hour. Hamper laid most of the blame for the malaise at the feet of the management and as we drove past the giant GM Institute building he talked bitterly about "the Pinheads and the Bifocal set" who were trained there to be "Kaisers and bossmen". They were taught management techniques but were never shown how to turn a screw; then they were sent to be in charge of forty guys who had been doing the job for ten years. He told me in a mixture of rage and laughter about a ploy used by the management when he was at GM. They recruited a worker to dress up as a cat called Howie Makem (geddit?), walk round the plant with a large "Q" emblazoned on his chest and preach about quality. It took a while, but eventually the workers realised how deeply demeaning this was to them, and soon Howie not only had a "Q" on his chest but a selection of rivets on his back. Eventually the cat didn't come back. As a worker Hamper reckoned he was employed by "bottom line people". The work was awful but if it was done adequately the management did not care what workers got up to. "They would not care if you strapped a tampon to your head, walked upside down in a dress and ran crack."

We passed the purple hulk of the Truck Division facility where

Hamper had worked and beside it the bar called Mark's Lounge where he had spent much off-, and on-, duty time. He talked about the bleakness of the place now and the huge social costs of the lack of jobs. People had either left Flint or taken demeaning minimum-wage jobs while many grown men had to swallow pride and go back to live with their parents. There still wasn't much to look forward to for these people because the axe never stopped falling. The GM engine plant which had a reputation as one of the best facilities in the Corporation was scheduled to be mothballed in '93 taking with it another 10,000 precious jobs. It was difficult for Hamper to make any gags about that.

On the way back from the GM plant we drove past a large deserted complex of buildings in the centre of Flint with a massive car park around them. This was not another empty car factory but another example of the disastrous thinking at the top of the auto industry. AutoWorld was a theme park based on the history of the car which was built at a cost of $80 million in the mid-Eighties. It was a mistake from the start and only lasted a couple of years because there were never enough people who wanted to come. What upset Hamper most was the arrogance of building a tribute to the technology which was destroying a community, right in the centre of that community. There was one display which made even a meek, mild-mannered man like him seethe. It was a tribute to the brave new technology revolutionising the industry and featured a model of a man, obviously with time on his hands, playing the banjo while serenading a working robot spot welder. The man was actually singing to the machine which had cost him his job. Hamper told me that all he wanted to do was to leap over the barrier and "beat the shit out of the display". I would've helped. We drove back to Hamper's house which was also his factory now. The shop rat had become a full-time writer and was now working on his second book. I still got the impression he slightly preferred a rivet gun to a typewriter but in this town he was lucky to have an option.

So Detroit had lost a large mainly white section of its population, had lost much of its key industrial base and hundreds of thousands of jobs, had even lost Motown Records which had moved to Los Angeles, but had not lost hope. It was clear that Detroit was not choked by the kind of despair which flowed like slime through the streets of East St Louis. The city had always had a cultural energy which had sustained it through the dark days, and music and art were obviously as important as ever. The local listings magazines were crammed with events happening in town but, sadly, I only had time to go to one place while I was there. It was the Detroit Institute of the Arts which I had passed on my drive down Woodward, the fifth largest gallery in America and much of it a gift from the multi-millionaires of the auto industry. From gratitude or guilt, I wondered?

I went out down Woodward again and was shown round by a local artist who happened to have a piece hanging in the gallery. Gilda Snowden was a talented young black woman from Detroit who had chosen to stay in her home town to teach and work. She accepted the problems of the place but believed in the future, particularly with a new liberal Administration in office. Talking to her was a vibrant antidote to the harsh economics of Detroit in the Nineties. Snowden proudly showed me her work on display in the gallery, a large and energetic bright-red collage called "Monument" which was a tribute to her parents. Fortunately for our new-found friendship I loved it.

Snowden insisted on taking me to see the centre piece of the Institute, the Detroit Industry Frescoes by Diego Rivera, which she said I would really like. Diego Rivera was an inspired Mexican muralist who was commissioned in 1932 to decorate two walls of the Institute's high-ceilinged Garden Court. The theme was to be the history of Detroit and the development of industry and Rivera prepared for the job by spending time at Ford's Rouge Industrial complex. So captivated was he by what he saw there that he asked to work on all four walls and by March 1933 had produced twenty-seven stunning panels, a combination of his love of machines and the men who made them against a background of the influence of industry on the natural world. The brilliance of the work is only matched by the rigour of its creation. Frescoes have to be painted on wet plaster and Rivera had only from eight to sixteen hours to complete a section. He did have assistants but performed most of the work himself and lost a hundred pounds in the process.

When the frescoes were revealed for the first time there was uproar because of what people saw. Some thought industry was not a fit subject for art, some thought the nudes were pornographic, some thought a vaccination scene was sacrilegious, and many worried that his Marxist views showed through. However, 4,000 local people signed a petition to prevent the frescoes being whitewashed and they were saved. As the controversy died in Detroit Rivera began the Rockefeller Center mural in New York, a work which was destroyed before it was completed because it included a painting of Lenin. Thank God the small-minded did not get their way in Detroit because a great work of art would have been lost. I stood in the centre of the hall drinking in the brilliance of Rivera and shared in his critical celebration of the industrial age. It would have taken days to take in everything drawn on those walls but in my short time I could enjoy the vitality of the Ford workers Rivera had captured and sealed on plaster. They reminded me of the drawings of the Clyde shipbuilders by Stanley Spencer which I love. Art, Nature and Engineering in one room, but no scones.

Chapter Eight

Massillon, Ohio
and the Catskills, New York State

It may have come to your attention that there had been precious little time on this journey for the author to stop and "chill out" as they like to call it in those parts. When I wasn't driving I was eating, when I wasn't eating I was sleeping, and when I wasn't sleeping I was just a terrible person to be around ... The schedule, which was the polite name for a regime crafted for me by a sadist, meant that I had very little chance to put on my slippers and settle down in front of the television. And for that I would always be grateful. It was a cliched thing to say, but it was even more true on this trip than any time I had been in America before. American television really was, not to put to fine a point on it, crap and the only sensible thing to do about it was not to watch. Ever. If sixty-four channels all showing shite is the result of deregulated television then Britain was in big trouble. The much-vaunted American network news coverage had the same intellectual content as *Hello!* magazine and amongst the wall-to-wall pap I could find no shows which dealt with anything approaching real life. The schedules were aimed at brain-dead couch potatoes who were not in possession of a life and craved hours of endless daytime television filled with talk shows featuring lesbian weightlifters who had raped their mothers. The only interesting thing about those awful voyeuristic programmes was the reaction of the studio audiences, which taught me a lot about the way contemporary America thinks. If I could sum up, American women hate men and American men want to be Burt Reynolds. I do worry about Americans, sometimes.

What American television does do very well is sport. Networks have realised that they can take news and political coverage as down-market as they want, and cheapen all drama into nonstop tawdry soap opera but they can't mess around with the most critical element of American life: the inalienable right of an American citizen to purchase a six-pack of beer and slump in a chair to watch the ball game. It's as American as apple pie and throughout my journey I had noticed that sport seemed to be last thing left that Americans really cared about. They were all very different, these Americans, but they shared a powerful patriotism which found its best expression in sport (outside times when they were "kicking some ass" in the Persian Gulf). Sport is not a thing *some* people do, rather it is shared by every member of the family, community and society. Sport has become the single most effective way of defining everything else because it is so universally understood. Politicians describe their policies using sports analogies, generals sound like American football coaches, and preachers offer a life game-plan endorsed by the Head Coach in the sky. To completely understand America I realised you had to understand their attitude to sport. It was time to go to the ball game.

I had travelled through America at a time when it was difficult for some Americans to lead any semblance of a normal life because of the intensity of sport on television. Late Fall into Winter is dominated at the highest level by the Baseball World Series and the National Football League season which exists primarily to give America something to talk about and fill hundreds of hours of television time. During that October

the Toronto Blue Jays had become the first non-American team to win the World Series, baseball's biggest prize, and America had been rocked on its heels by the victory. The fact that the Blue Jays did not have a single Canadian national playing for them was immaterial, the sporting manhood of America had been challenged and found wanting. And that had got the viewing manhood of America angry, so next time their boys better win or they might switch off. The message had been received and understood by all concerned.

What really defined the American way of sport was much further down the line from the multi-millionaire players of major league baseball and the NFL. The obsession stretched right down through the descending levels of competitive sport in a way that I could not come to terms with. I decided to investigate and left Detroit to drive south and east towards Akron (Rubber Capital of the World), then a bit further south to a small town called Massillon, Ohio which I had been told was the football craziest in the whole of America. I wanted to go to a football game where the fans really were fanatics to get a fix on the unnatural hold the sport has over sane human beings. Massillon is a small Ohio town of around 30,000 souls. It has no professional sports team or even a gifted senior amateur team, but it does have a stadium which holds 20,000 people and which would be completely full the next day. Incredibly, the team which two thirds of the town's population would be turning up to watch was the local High School Football team. It wasn't like that for the Primary Six Second Eleven at Auchenshuggle Primary, I can tell you.

Every year the crunch game for Massillon High was the local derby game against a team from the larger town of Canton just up the road. It did not matter what kind of a season it had been for Massillon because the definition of a good year was one in which they hammered Canton McKinley, and to make sure that darned possibility called defeat didn't get in the way of a good party the fans held a parade and celebration the night *before* the big game. I got into town just as the festivities were starting in the main street of Massillon. The whole town was there and all appeared to be wearing orange. Massillon's team were called the Tigers and Canton's were the Bulldogs but this was the night of the Tiger; and when I saw a policeman in uniform with an orange tail hanging from his arse, I realised just how seriously it was being taken. The parade was made up of a lengthy stream of cars and vans painted in orange, carrying local celebrities such as Amy-Louise, better known as Miss Downtown Massillon. The people in the cars threw sweets at the people watching and everyone had a whale of a time. A whole fleet of limos drove past carrying the team coaches, and then the Tigers rolled into view. They looked a mean bunch of sixteen-year-old psychopaths, sporting the worst haircuts I had seen in a long time. Didn't matter under a helmet, I suppose. The excitement and spectacle were already greater than for most British sports events and the game was still eighteen hours away. I spoke to some locals who explained that the rivalry between the two teams stretched back ninety-eight years, which made it the oldest in America. It had been a disappointing season for the Tigers but it would all be alright if they "stomped the pups" the next day. The parade passed, rocking to the sound of a fantastic Swing band from the school, who compensated for the awfulness of their polyester uniforms by playing some fab foot-tappers. Massillon partied long into the night but with an innocent kind of jollity which contrasted markedly with British sports fans tanking up for a game. The only violence there was going to be was on the pitch and all strictly legal. I raised a glass to their Corinthian spirit.

Match day was bitterly cold with snow blowing in the air as I parked the Cadillac behind the stands of Paul Brown Tiger Stadium. The arena was much more comfortable than many British football grounds, in fact it was more comfortable than many British houses. I settled down to watch the build-up and enjoy the novelty of a sports crowd of nearly 20,000 made up of families with children having fun. I forced down four hot dogs, just to be sociable, and began to understand what it was that sport means to Americans. It gives them a sense of identity and a celebration of important values. It is possibly the last collective community experience left and brings people together for a positive purpose. Forgive me, I was just feeling that, if you like, I had "caught the sport ball and was about to run with it" when a terrible thing happened. The game started.

Two things to say. Firstly, no matter how much hype and expectation is invested in a football game involving spotty sixteen-year-old school-boys, they are always going to be just boys with acne, not professional athletes. The players, despite looking like pros with all their equipment, were generally poor at the game and play tended to be littered with mistakes. Secondly, I found that I hated American football and decided it was no more than rugby with the grace extracted. Each team had huge numbers of players on the sidelines (about fifty a side, just in case) and the action only ever lasted ten seconds at a time and ended in what looked like a car crash. The game stopped so often it was like the torture of watching a good movie with hundreds of commercials. I'll stick with rugby, if you don't mind.

My feelings were not shared by the fans around me in the stadium who had been whipping themselves into a frenzy of anticipation as the kick-off got closer. When the game did start I noticed that the atmosphere suddenly became curiously passionless, almost sterile. It was as though the crowd had been exhausted by the intensity of the pre-match hype and had decided that the best time to recover was during the match in question. The mood was not helped by the fact that the Bulldogs quickly began stomping on the Tigers, something which the people of Massillon had assumed was not in the script. A few brave souls in the street had whispered to me that Massillon were not a great side this

year and they were being proved absolutely right. Massillon had the fans, the live tiger mascot, the cutest cheerleaders, the history, the stadium. McKinley had the lead. The local lads always seemed to come off worst in the car crashes and through the metal grilles on their helmets I could see on their faces that many of them wished they had taken a few more driving lessons. McKinley cruised to a 14–6 victory, with their No Claims Bonus still intact.

At the full-time whistle the crowd was getting up to go home when an extraordinary thing happened on the field which horrified the watching thousands. Fans had run on to the pitch to engage, I would suppose, in witty banter about the success or failure of their favourites. Then in a flash Massillon was transformed into Millwall and some of those fans seemed to be scuffling on the field; the atmosphere had turned uncharacteristically ugly. There was a brief rumble then a man went down injured and the police, caught unawares like everyone else, got on the field and caught a tough-looking young guy. It was a very brief incident of soccer-style ugliness but it shattered a popular image of American sports fans. I discovered later that the injured man was the father of one of the Massillon players and he was fine after a check-up. The guy who hit him was also from Massillon so it was probably just a stupid blow-up in the heat of the moment. I would say it was the most exciting thing I saw all day but I would be a liar. I didn't actually see the incident because I had left the ground a long time before because ... I had heard there was some paint drying in another part of town.

The next day I was feeling like the majority of the people of Massillon, that I never wanted to see another football game in my entire life. The difference between us was that they would all go to the next game and I really would never see another football game. That gave me a good feeling as I headed out of town, turned right onto the 76 to Youngstown, Ohio then followed the 80 through the state of Pennsylvania. The air smelt of the East and the magic words New and York had started to appear together on Interstate signs. I was under 350 miles away from the Promised Land and the Cadillac was going like a dream. Unfortunately,

I had just discovered that she was not stopping so effortlessly. The Peterbilt truck (and are they cute, or is Scammel an aftershave?) a distance ahead of me on the Interstate flashed red for an instant and slowed down, so I touched my brakes. I was going about 55 mph and I felt an icy hand grasp my gut as the brake pedal went all the way to the floor and nothing happened. I pumped the pedal again but there was no response. This was our old friend "total brake failure" and I knew that I was in big trouble. Welcome to Brown Trouser country. Trust me, this book would not have been written if the Interstate had been even a little bit busier that day. Luckily, the gaps on the road gave me the room to slow the car down with the transmission then use the parking brake to stop on the hard shoulder. If I had been tail-gating the truck as I had done occasionally before, then it would have been goodnight, Vienna and a rather sad end to the third part of my four-programme documentary series. It also would have meant a slight problem for programme four, content wise. I suspected that the Cadillac had picked up a hole in the main brake pipe, which turned out to be exactly the problem. I had to wait around for a pick-up truck to take the Cadillac to a garage off the Interstate but I was happy just to sit doing nothing for a while. I think I had gone into a sort of shock. The last time I remembered feeling like that was when I read my schedule for this trip.

What with everything happening and all the strain and pressure on me, I decided that I needed a break before going to New York. I deserved a little time, a little oasis in the Desert of the Eternal Freeway, to recharge my battery (and check my brakes). I knew exactly the place where I could grab myself some Quality Time and it was on my way. I continued east through the rolling forests of Pennsylvania, through Scranton, and crossed into NEW YORK State at Port Jervis. New York, so good I wrote it in capital letters. Then north-east on Route 42 through a winter wonderland of snowy, densely wooded hills, past Monticello and on to South Fallsburg. This was the heart of the world-famous Catskill Mountains and I had arrived in the Borscht Belt, the area which has been the country playground of Jewish New Yorkers for years and the breeding ground for generations of the best comedians. And the worst.

The Borscht Belt had started around the turn of the century when boarding houses called *Kochelein*, Yiddish for "communal kitchen", sprang up in the Catskills to cater for the influx of Jews escaping the hell of New York's garment district. Over the years American anti-Semitism turned those small boarding houses into huge hotels as Jewish holidaymakers, unwelcome elsewhere, flocked to the Catskills. The golden days were in the Fifties when Cadillacs like the one I was driving would have been parked in the drives of over five hundred hotels in the area. Now there were just five main resort hotels and around fifty smaller places to cater for the much smaller market. The Catskills' popularity had waned for several reasons. The growth of the suburbs and the spread of air-conditioning meant it was less vital to get away from the city in the summer, and the gradual lessening of anti-semitism had opened up more places for Jews. Now the clientele was older and not exclusively Jewish, particularly outside holidays and summertime. It was even possible to get non-kosher food in the Catskills these days, and the whole diner would not now go silent if you ever asked for a bacon cheeseburger. To me the Catskills spelt comedy and it was in the big Show Rooms of the top hotels where names like Danny Kaye, Sid Caesar, Mel Brooks, and a short guy with glasses called Woody Allen got their first breaks sharpening the kind of material which has influenced every comic since. Those days have gone, but I wanted to see if the memories lingered on.

I had chosen the Raleigh, pronounced *Rawlly*, as my resort hotel. It was not the largest in the Catskills but it did have 800 rooms arranged in a sprawling collection of varied architectural styles and all the facilities expected of a Catskills resort: nightclub, pool, mini-golf, and paramedics. The matching white of the exterior of the main building and the inch of snow on the ground was a poor preparation for the explosion of colour inside the lobby. Orange and gilt had been particular favourites of the interior designer: the general look of the decor was Faded Vegas Vulgar. The map of the hotel at the front desk showed how the Raleigh had grown over the years, sprouting wings and towers when business was good. I had a sneaking desire to be put in the Old Sammy Davis Wing because I liked the name but they gave me a room in Kennedy Towers instead. Surely he wasn't Jewish?

I could see that I was at least thirty years younger than the rest of the guests and, from the interest I provoked, I guessed they did not get too many large, relatively youthful Scotsmen stopping by. I found out later that the management had arranged a special showing the day before of *Nuns on the Run* when they heard I was coming to stay. Several residents took the time to compliment me on how good I looked in a dress. At my age, that's important.

I had arrived on Tuesday, November 17th and was now an official part of a Senior Citizens Midweek Break. A closely typed sheet of A4 had been thrust into my hand which revealed that every millisecond of a Raleigh day was organised. The people who came to the hotel worked hard at taking it easy and I supposed I would have to as well. I checked the schedule for Wednesday and selected some highlights:

9:30 am	Psychic reading lecture
10:00 am	Yoga Relaxation with Bebe
11:00 am	Line dancing with Bebe
2:00 pm	Bingo
3:15 pm	Talent Show with Jack
3:30 pm	Aquanastics
6:00 pm	Lavish Smorgasbord Cocktail Party
9:30 pm	Showtime

I was impressed but not fooled. I actually knew that all these activities were just an elaborate smokescreen for the real purpose of a visit to the Catskills: eating. That, an authority had told me knowingly, was the only thing people cared about. "They check in as guests and check out as cargo. They don't need bellhops, they need forklifts..." The food

never stopped and there seemed to be only very short periods when I was outside the enormous dining room. Each meal was huge but dinner was spectacular. Six courses with a choice of six entrées and six desserts made up the standard menu. Dining was organised with military precision and by the kind of Latin American waiter who speeded up the operation by making up *his* mind what you were having today. Each table seemed to hold twelve small people with loud voices who all knew each other, and I worried that it would not be easy being a lone traveller and diner. Barry Frank, a tiny fast-talking man who was Mr Entertainment at the hotel, insisted on ushering me to a table with only eleven small people and sat me down there. My dining companions were all women of a certain age who made me welcome in an abrasive sort of way. They were unimpressed by the scale of my epic journey and the work I did for a living, but they were impressed by the Shadow Laker Cake which had been baked on the premises. I was looking forward to it too but I must have blinked at ordering time and so discovered good old José had chosen the Pastry Palm Leaves for me, bless him. I chatted to the ladies while we battled through the mountains of food which appeared at incredible speed and we covered many topics: the correct use of napkins in a restaurant, the historic derivation of the surnames at the table, the National Health Service, and the Jewish approach to Christmas. All very interesting but I really wanted to steer the conversation round to comedy and hear their thoughts about Jewish humour. One of the women seized the initiative and told me that she had something important to say about the subject. "That Roseanne Arnold [Jewish comedy actress who happened to be brought up in Salt Lake City], she's not Jewish," the woman said angrily to me. "Have you seen her house [meaning the set of the highly successful series *Roseanne*]? No Jewish woman would have a house look like that. *I'd* be ashamed to have a house look like that..." I choked on my baked corned beef and changed the subject.

Comedy was still on the menu at the Raleigh but the days of haute cuisine had long gone. Everything was still kosher, of course. I caught the afternoon Talent Show going on in the bar as I recovered from the calorie assault of lunch and quickly got the flavour of the material the punters liked. I arrived as a very elderly lady was reaching the climax of her joke. The last line involved the word "pussy", and we're not talking Felix here. Whatever, it brought the house down and was only topped when the host, a cadaverous comic called Jack Dibo (who happened to be the husband of Entertainment Director Bebe Dibo) told a long predictable joke about an old man joining a nudist club. There was not a dry seat in the room after that one. That night I thought I should see a professional at work so I settled down in the Raleigh nightclub to watch Van Harris do his set. Harris was a thin, intense guy in his sixties who had been around the scene for years. His comedy revolved around the twin Jewish obsessions of bad health and European roots and he cleverly drew the audience into his world. He was from Brooklyn (he got a round for mentioning the fact), was definitely playing on home turf, and the routines he built out of his Russian immigrant heritage brought sighs of recognition as well as laughter. A simple story about how his father had learned English allowed Harris to make a slightly racist comment about the immigrants of today not making an effort to learn the language (tumultuous applause), and tell a twee tale about his father calling Idaho potatoes "Hidey Hole potatoes" (biggest laugh of the night). The audience, which had an average age of about seventy, also loved gags like, "I was playing golf and I got out of a sand trap with one stroke. Is that good? [big pause] My doctor says if I have another stroke..." Boom boom. His comedy was really holding a mirror up to the audience, and sharing similar hopes, fears, and haemorrhoids. It reminded me in a way of Glasgow humour: a nice build-up with a punchline always designed to undercut the expectations of the audience. I wonder who did it first? Och, I should worry.

I had (several) drinks with Van Harris after the show, sitting at a small table in the deserted nightclub. He had changed from his stage suit into a casual jacket with open-necked shirt and there were dark shadows under his eyes. He talked about the days when he was starting out and "the Social Directors were kings but the performers were treated like garbage." They were hard times, with so many shows every week Harris had to take suitcases filled with material rather than suits while outside the local police used to be so anti-Semitic they tried to ticket as many Jews on their way to the Catskills as they could. He talked about the great successes the system had thrown up, with performers like Danny Kaye, and writers like Woody Allen and Neil Simon working the hotels, but admitted that the conveyor belt had stopped. The audience had changed and the increasing numbers of Christian guests found some of the self-deprecating Jewish humour too hard to take so it was a case of adapt and survive. The world had changed and the owners now spent less money on the shows and their performers. Harris talked about the Catskills in the Nineties with a kind of forced confidence. "It's still the best value vacation you can get," he was saying as someone switched off the power in the empty nightclub and we were plunged into darkness. "Much better than Vegas." You didn't have to be a semiologist to catch the symbolism.

I loved my time in the Catskills. The place and the people made my couple of days feel like I'd been at a family wedding with lots of nice sentiment and constant jollification with old codgers. This area used to be the place the smart set went to have affairs in the Fifties, but now it was really just somewhere elderly Jewish people who hadn't gone to Florida ended up. There was a bit of a sad, slightly run-down feel to the Raleigh but that was part of the charm. Where would I rather stay, the Excalibur, Las Vegas or the Raleigh, South Fallsburg? Cut me a slice of that Shadow Laker Cake, José!

Chapter Nine

New York, New York

"Still movin', huh?" The words were shouted at me from the sidewalk as I drove the road-weary Cadillac the 3,674th mile of a 3,765-mile journey. If I had been in any other part of America I'd have thought, "Wise guy, huh?". However, because of where I was – I was cool and just gave an enigmatic shrug. Earlier that morning of the 19th of November I had driven south on the Palisades Interstate Parkway into the state of New Jersey and followed the west bank of the Hudson River to the George Washington Bridge. Then it happened as I had always wanted it to happen. I drove into New York, down the finger of Manhattan, in a beautiful black Cadillac; my favourite place in the whole world apart from Glasgow, which I'd always thought was very similar, being filled with the same quiet, restrained, passive, people. As I purred down the Hudson Parkway and cut across town at 46th Street it occurred to me that this time people would see the car and think I was somebody. Then that guy shouted from the sidewalk and reminded me that New Yorkers were not impressed by anything. I had to react with a couldn't-give-a-shit expression to show that even the driver was not impressed by the Cadillac. But we both knew that if deep down New Yorkers thought something was really cool then they would insult it, as the sidewalk Joe had done. The Cadillac was cool on 46th Street. And any other street you'd care to mention.

New York was at her very best, with the marble and glass formations of Manhattan looking even more dazzling than the best Southern Utah could offer. I could almost smell the electricity in the air. I was back in the world's most exciting city and probably the world's most dangerous city in which to leave a Classic Cadillac on the street overnight. I had got this far in one piece and was worried that the guy coming to pick up the Caddy on Saturday to take it to New Jersey for shipping might have a wasted journey. It turned out not to be a problem. I was staying at the Paramount Hotel on 46th Street, just off Broadway and Times Square, and there was a car park across the street run by some nice Italian boys. They liked the Cadillac so much they forgot to be cool about it. They would look after the car like she was their "bambino" and nothing would happen to her. Maybe Florence was nearer than I thought.

I had just driven across the whole of the United States but no part of my journey could prepare me for being in Gotham again. I felt a kind of culture shock at the sheer intensity of the city going on around me. I lived here off and on for a couple of years back around 1980 and loved the experience, but the city had got darker since then. It used to be that there were a few bad parts of town but now it seemed that every part of town was a bad part of town. The gun culture which I had seen right across America combined with the craziness of New York made for an explosive mixture which tended to go off in the faces of innocent passers-by. So whaddaya gonna do? Spend all your life in Des Moines?

I had an important appointment that Thursday evening. I was due to speak to the people of America (aye, Robbie, that'll be right...). Absolutely true, because I had been invited to appear on the most famous and

popular night-time talk show on national television, NBC's *Late Night With David Letterman* to shoot the breeze with Dave about my cross-country trip. This was not my first time on the show and in fact I'd done it a couple of times in the last few months. Letterman liked you if you were funny and I'd already had a phone conversation with a researcher trying to drag amusing anecdotes about the journey from me. I don't know why they bother because those stories never make it on to the show, but doing talk shows is a game and they like it if you play by their rules. The stretch limo arrived at the Paramount around 4.30 to take me the few blocks to the Rockefeller Center where the NBC New York Studios are based in the Forties splendour of the General Electric Building. The *Letterman Show* was recorded at 5.30 and aired across America at around midnight. David Letterman is a former stand-up comedian from Muncie, Indiana who has been doing the show for over ten years and was at that time in negotiation to go to another network for ten million dollars. Nice work, if you can get it.

My fellow guests on the Thursday evening show were the band 10,000 Maniacs performing their new song, and some guy called Kevin Costner talking about a film. Kevin (or Kev as I call him) was the first on, followed by the band, then I was to close the show. What I was actually most looking forward to was hearing the resident house band led by Paul Shaeffer warm up the studio audience, because they are brilliant. The Letterman studio is purpose-built and quite compact so when Shaeffer turned up the amps the band really lifted the roof. The main backstage area of the show was a wide brightly lit corridor where all the artists and technicians hung around and I met Kevin Costner there and had a blether, as you do. He was on to promote his new movie with Whitney Houston called *The Bodyguard*. Kevin was desperate to find out how I always managed to look so handsome in the movies. He was very friendly and unstarry, but I had to say, "Kev, that's for me to know, and you to wonder about."

I waited for my moment. I knew that I would be on for about five minutes and in that time would have to make some kind of impression on seventeen million people. Also I was in a foreign country with an audience which would miss about half of what I was saying, so, theoretically, I had to be twice as entertaining. The researcher gave me a final piece of advice: "It's basically as conversational as you can make it. No yes/no answers..." Gee thanks.

The interview went fairly well and I think I managed fairly long sentences most of the time. Paul Shaeffer and the band played a piece of John Coltrane as I walked on and Letterman was in very good form. We talked about the highlights of the journey and the audience laughed a bit and I sweated a lot. They liked my description of the Cadillac as a mobile Radio City and my story (apocryphal) about the pump attendant filling the car with gas asking me to turn off the engine because he couldn't keep up. Letterman leant across during a break and said that he had done the trip himself about ten years ago. And then it was over and I was in the limo heading back to the Paramount. Some day maybe I would get a proper job...

I decided to catch up the next day with an old buddy of mine, a brilliant film director and all-round good guy named Amos Poe. Amos Poe was the man who put punk on the map with *Blank Generation*, *CBGB's*, and a host of deeply stylish *nouvelle vague* underground films. Earlier that year we had finished *Triple Bogey on A Par Five Hole*. Amos was the man to help me catch the New York mood and he said he had a couple of people I should meet. Breakfast near the Bowery was his suggestion so I trundled down in the Cadillac to a small red-brick building in the heart of one of New York's less respectable neighbourhoods, deep in the Lower East Side of Manhattan. The Bowery is an old thoroughfare which runs past Chinatown, Little Italy, SoHo, and Greenwich Village, and it has declined into a kind of Skid Row for the less fortunate citizens of the city. We met at the Jones Diner on Lafayette and Third, which used to be one of our favourite haunts, and I was pleased to find the coffee was still as hot as the cheek from the staff. Over our eggs Amos introduced me to a man with a slight accent and a pair of round specs. Luc Santé is a Belgian who has lived in New York

for twenty years and has become fascinated with the seamier side of life in the city. So much so that he has written an acclaimed book called *Low Life* about the underside of New York. He had been inspired, he told me, because he had lived in the Bowery area when he first came to New York and had been surrounded by, as he put it, "all sorts of semi-bad shit going on" (this boy could be a wow writing for *Hello!*, I thought). He went on to trace in detail the history of this place which has become synonymous with bad boys and bad behaviour. Luc suggested we take a morning constitutional on the street to see how low life still was out there.

The Bowery was originally a farm road when Manhattan was a Dutch colony and taverns sprang up on it to cater for the farmers. As New York grew so did the badness on the Bowery and by the early 1900's both sides of the road were filled with bars serving three-cents whisky, flop-houses, dime-a-dance halls, amusement arcades, and whore-houses. Sounds absolutely horrid, doesn't it? At its peak, the Bowery had more bars than anywhere else in New York with eighty-five on the East Side but only twenty on the West. Nobody has ever been able to explain the reason for the disparity. In the early days of the movies when the medium was frowned upon by decent people, the Nickelodeon owners had to come to the Bowery to open their theatres, and no less than D.W. Griffith filmed there too. As we strolled on the grubby sidewalks, Santé pointed out buildings with interesting stories, like the notorious Barbers' Academies where a New Yorker could get the worst haircut in town, but cheap, and McGurk's Suicide Hall which had got its name after a number of prostitutes decided to end their miserable lives by ingesting carbolic acid in the middle of the dance floor. McGurk was an enterprising businessman and cashed in on the sordid tragedy by adding the S word to the title of the hall, making much of the implication that it might happen again. Sure enough, macabre people with a warped sense of entertainment flocked there every night hoping for a replay.

The Bowery looked very run-down now with its decrepit buildings and people, but Santé said there was a kind of regeneration happening

off it, especially around Chinatown where Hong Kong emigrés were coming in with money and converting the buildings. Nothing ever stands still in this town for long.

We ambled back to the diner passing hundreds of shops full of pizza-makers, bagel-makers, mozzarella-crushers and all the shiny paraphernalia of the mysteries of catering. John Manniel was sitting there with a small cup of coffee and a big attitude. He was a lean, obviously very fit man in his fifties with a blond crewcut and a black outfit which had a large golden eagle embroidered on the back. He had the dull eyes of someone who has seen a lot of life, much of which he has not liked, but he greeted Amos with affection. It turned out Manniel was an extraordinary character, and certainly the most remarkable guy I had met on my travels. He had been a New York Police Department cop for twenty years and Amos told me the only way he could think of describing Manniel was as a cross between Batman and Serpico. I bought him another coffee, then he suggested we go to his 'hood.

The Brooklyn Bridge is one of the most spectacular pieces of design and engineering in the whole of New York. Only in New York could there be a Gothic suspension bridge. Its graceful sweeping span links Lower Manhattan with Brooklyn over the East River, and Manniel talked to me under the Brooklyn side of the bridge. It was the definitive (alright, clichéd) New York location with a stunning view of the cramped tip of Manhattan where the giant towers jostle for space in a jungle of concrete. Off in the distance the Statue of Liberty, in contrast, seemed to have all the room in the world on her lonely island out in the wide reaches of Upper Bay. It was afternoon now and the city glittered in the low November sun, the twin towers of the World Trade Center shining like chrome against the watery blue sky. Traffic poured over the bridge way above our heads but it was strangely peaceful where we stood. Brooklyn was Manniel's territory and the only place he felt truly comfortable. He told me his story.

He was born John Francis Manniel, the son of an Irish father and Sicilian mother, fifty-two years ago in Brooklyn, and worked in the

music business as a young man. He claimed to have written 800 songs which he recorded under the name of Johnny Mann and also with a band called Eric and the Vikings. He tried his hand at managing rock bands but show business was never going to be the right place for his unique talents and he only found his true vocation when he applied to join the Police Department. There turned out to be a slight problem with his suitability to don a blue uniform because most of his relatives on his mother's side were in a Sicilian family business - *the* Sicilian Family business. The Department were worried about taking on a man who regularly mixed with Mob members, but Manniel threatened to sue them if he was not allowed in. "I don't tell my uncles how to make a living, they don't tell me. If I had wanted to go that way I would have done." He eventually got on the force after a three-year battle and became the white sheep of his family. His Italian uncles, incredibly, were very proud of him and he continued to see them at family occasions. Sometimes he would get a call from Headquarters because some FBI guy tailing one of his family had seen his car outside a known Mob house and called the police wondering what one of their officers was doing there.

Manniel was never an ordinary policeman. It did not take him long on the street to realise that conventional police methods were not very effective in the battle against crime, particularly gang crime which was rife in Brooklyn. His beat was in the mainly Latino section where the gangs ruled the neighbourhood by fear and he decided the only way to counteract them was by waging his own personal war against them. He became a Ninja Assassin, a lone vigilante dressed in black with a Ninja mask who took the law into his own hands to inflict justice on the gangs. It sounded like a Steven Seagal screenplay, but it was real and highly effective as he used his skill in Martial Arts and his knowledge of the streets to hunt down the gangs and make them pay for their crimes. He told me the story of the time a deaf mute girl was dragged into a gang clubhouse by some members and brutally raped. The rapists were caught and even picked out by the girl in an identification parade but she would not go through with filing a complaint against them because she was so terrified about possible retribution against her and her family. Manniel was in the station as this happened and he watched the gang members smiling and laughing because they had beaten the rap. They stopped celebrating when he told them in front of the District Attorney that they would have to face *his* justice. It started with a little harassment when Manniel broke into their clubhouse and left glass in their boots and Mace on their pillows. Then their clubhouse had a mysterious fire and burnt to the ground leaving the gang out on the streets in the middle of winter. The gang found another house and somehow it burnt down too. The gang eventually lost their will to continue and broke up. The poor girl had some kind of justice.

Manniel fought the gangs singlehanded and seemingly without fear. He said that he had only drawn his gun once in his career and it had misfired at that moment. He liked to challenge the gangs when he met them in uniform and tell them to get off the streets. Gang members would taunt him about hiding behind his gun and badge and he would suggest they meet in Sunset Park when he was off duty. There would be maybe eighteen of them there and Manniel would offer to take them out three at a time. "Eighteen on one, you got me, but you'd better fuckin' kill me because when I get out of hospital I'm gonna come back for you." His strategy was to kick the ass of the guy with the loudest voice and then one other and they would all fall into line, "like chickens following their mother".

Manniel set up a karate school in the neighbourhood where he trained hundreds of street kids to become Black Belts and have the same discipline and confidence on the streets as he had. None of his students has ever been arrested and they became a sort of private army which protected him wherever he went. They also provided Manniel with the intelligence information he needed to do his work. Some of his students were related to gang members and through them he would hear about shoot-outs and robberies that were about to happen. He also liked to climb over the rooftops of the neighbourhood to find out where the gangs were hiding, and his intuitive knowledge of their movements started the rumour there were seven John the Cops out there. He knew how the gang members thought and could use his street psychology for maximum effect. He told me he had been involved in an arrest of sixteen boys and, instead of taking them away in cars, he got as many handcuffs as he could find, chained the sixteen in a line and walked them through the streets. Humiliation is always more effective than a fine.

Manniel said the definition of a Ninja was an invisible assassin but he had never killed anyone. "I'm an invisible ballbreaker. I didn't kill anyone, I just broke balls." There were many people who would have liked to see him in his box, of course, and over his career police intelligence picked up word of fourteen contracts with his name on them. Only one really worried him, "a professional fifteen-thousand-dollar job, five grand up front and the rest when the job was done." He found out who the hit man was and later "some Ninja guy dressed in black chopped all his fingers off with a twenty-six-inch Ninja blade. Guy with no fingers doesn't pull any triggers." He said he never killed anyone because that put them out of their misery. "But if you retard them a little, maybe some kind of injury which gives them arthritic pain, every time they get that pain they'll think of John Manniel, and hate you for the rest of their life."

The Police Department never liked Manniel's methods but they turned a blind eye as long as he kept clean. The Chief of Police once praised him for the work he had done in breaking up the gangs and said he would always try to protect him but told Manniel that if he ever messed up with his unconventional methods and got any unfavourable publicity the conversation they were having had never happened and he would be in deep trouble. He did make the front cover of the *New York Post* once but it was entirely favourable. "Karate Cop Zaps Gunman" was the headline and he became a media star for a while, to the even greater annoyance of his colleagues whose conventional police methods

were being shown up. He always went his own way in the force, constantly refusing the chance of promotion because he did not want to be at a desk and, coincidentally, he once worked with another famous lone-wolf New York cop, Frank Serpico. "We were on the Pussy

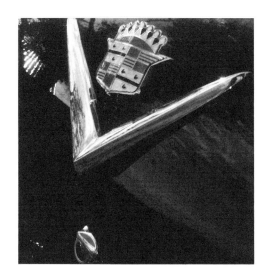

Posse together," which is NYPD slang for the Vice Squad. He was glad to be out of uniform now and enjoyed being free to do what he wanted.

It was getting dark and Manniel had to go. Just before he headed off into the Brooklyn gloom I asked him why he had a golden eagle on the back of his jacket. He laughed. "I'm the Golden Eagle of karate. When a pigeon flies by and shits on your head it's just a little bit, but when an eagle shits on your head it's rough." Barbara Cartland couldn't have put it better.

John Manniel was like a character from a comic, a super-powered Ninja warrior dedicated to fighting the power of evil on the streets of a ravaged city, but he had also talked worrying sense about crime in New York. The widely held view was that Los Angeles had the organised gangs which divided up their territory and ruled it with Uzi automatic weapons while New York had plenty of crime but no large organised-gang problem. Manniel had been committed to wiping out the smaller street gangs of his neighbourhood but he said that he was hearing word that New York had a coming problem like Los Angeles. The two biggest LA gangs, the Bloods and the Cripps, had now come to Harlem and he believed that if they were to get anywhere near the power of their Southern Californian brothers there would be mayhem on the New York streets. These were the gangs who killed people for nothing more than wearing the wrong "colors", the badges of gang membership. Manniel felt that the authorities were not taking the threat seriously enough and something needed to be done now. Meanwhile the Mob, he said, were reining back and no longer the power they used to be in New York. There were still places where senior figures could be seen sitting in state with young guys kissing their rings but the threat was much reduced. He also talked about his former partners in the police force, which had been wiped almost clean of corruption a few years before, and the problems they must have staying clean now when there was so much big drug money flying around the city. He left it at that.

Manniel painted a grim picture of New York in the Nineties and he was the kind of man who would know what was really happening out on the mean streets. What the city needed was another man like him, leading a normal existence in the daytime but transforming at night into a figure dressed in black who fought a lone war for truth and justice, using superhuman strength and courage, and with a winged creature as a symbol. How about ... a bat? And he could be called ... ManBat. Just a thought.

The date was etched on my brain. Saturday, November 21st, the day she left me. Together for four and a half weeks, sharing all the trials and tribulations of life on the road. Then she was gone. And with another guy.

He arrived at the Paramount on the Saturday morning to pick her up, a short guy with a baseball cap. (Actually, I don't know why I should use a baseball cap as a point of description because every single American male has one attached to his head. It's as hopeless as identifying someone as "a guy with a nose..." And why do Americans wear baseball caps? It is certainly not to shield the sun from their eyes as a high-fly ball from José Canseco comes out of the sky towards them in center field of Yankee Stadium, with the bases loaded, tied at the bottom of the seventh. No siree, Bob. They wear a cap because it has become a part of the uniform of their nationality, a badge of their pride in being American, and ... erm ... a marketing opportunity. And they hardly ever take them off. I remember back in an Ohio truckstop seeing about fifty bare-headed truckers at formica tables eating trucker food and realising all of them had those rings around their heads left by those attractive, "One size fits all" perforated nylon strips that adorn baseball caps.) Anyway, a blue baseball cap emblazoned with the legend "Giants" arrived, wearing a man who certainly wasn't.

The Cadillac had one final American journey to make. I drove her out of the car park onto 46th Street where the baseball cap had parked a flatbed truck in amongst the yellow Checker cabs and dented, hubcap-free automobiles which litter Manhattan. I watched as the car was winched onto the back of a truck which looked worryingly short and weak to carry such a precious load. "No problem," said the cap, unconvincingly. I handed over the keys, signed my name, and looked the cap straight in its brim. "You'll be very, very..." – I spoke with a quiet voice which I only brought out in the most special circumstances – "...very careful with this car. Won't you?" The brim moved up and down in a way which told me that the tone of my voice had been understood. There was a slight pause and then he climbed into the cab of his truck. I watched for a long time as the white roof of the car, unnaturally high on the back of the truck, disappeared into the dark canyons of Manhattan. The Cadillac was on her own. She went to the harbour at Port Elizabeth, New Jersey, sat there for a week or so, then was loaded aboard a cargo ship called the *Faust* (hadn't I given enough?) which set sail for Blighty on the 3rd of December and docked at Southampton on the 13th after eleven days on storm-tossed seas. Jezebel was home for Christmas.

I walked back to the hotel, a man alone with his memories in a city of eight million people. Perhaps I would steel myself, visit one of those dimly lit bars, and find out just how happy those Happy Hours could make me. I had done it. A 3,765-mile odyssey across the United States in the definitive American car, taking the most basic route in the book. Out of the Georgian hotel car park in Santa Monica, hang a right on Ocean Avenue, another right on Santa Monica Boulevard and follow your nose until you sniff another Ocean. I had travelled through thirteen states across every kind of terrain, in every kind of weather, and I had made it, on time and in one piece. The Great Adventure was over.

I kept walking until I hit the sidewalk of Broadway at Times Square. In the midst of thousands of grim-faced New Yorkers I wandered slowly down the Great White Way thinking about the America I had experienced on the trip. The contrasts were enormous: from the opulence of Beverly Hills to the abject poverty of East St Louis; from the decadent wildness of Las Vegas to the controlled austerity of the Amish; from the bitter cynicism of Detroit auto workers to the quiet dignity of Kansas farmers. The most extraordinary thing about the United States is the fact they are just that. United. There is a way there of allowing opposites to co-exist, bound together by a belief in one nation, one flag. They call it the "American Way". Unfortunately, I couldn't find anyone the length of the entire country who could explain what the American Way is.

The timing of my trip could not have come at a more critical point in the history of the States as I watched the electorate get the chance to change a political order which had seemed set in stone for so long. The superficiality of modern American political campaigning had made me positively homesick but I was still impressed by the genuine spirit Bill Clinton brought to his quest for the White House (even if he did like Fleetwood Mac). Stealing unashamedly from Kennedy, the saxophonist from Arkansas convinced the Americans he could give them a new beginning, and I was there to witness him being given his chance. Now he, and his supporters, could enjoy the glory of victory without having to worry about political reality until the 20th of January 1993. For a few weeks hope would be thick in the air in America, even on the mean streets of Midtown Manhattan.

It was time to go home. I turned back through the throng of New York humanity to go to the hotel to pack my bags. Later, in the cab to

JFK, I realised how hard it would be to encapsulate my impressions of 266 million people, and I knew I would be a fool to try, but my lasting impressions were of a nation which had had a severe loss of confidence and was slowly recovering. The truth is that everything that is good about America is wonderful and everything that is bad about America is atrocious. It occurred to me that perhaps, after all, that is the American Way.

There is an old Buddhist story about a traveller leaving a town. On the outskirts he meets a wise old man coming from the direction of the next town.

"Hey, old fellow! What are the people like in that town over there?" asks the traveller.

"Well," asks the wise man in return, "what did you think the people were like in the town you just left?"

"They were rude, thoughtless, selfish and showed me no kindness whatsoever."

"Then that is just how you will find the people in the town you are going to."

(Enigmatic or what?)

Acknowledgements

Thanks to the Tiger Television crew and the London team for helping to get us to the other side: Charles Brand, Stephen Smallwood, Paul Sommers, Mike Fox, Mike Lax, John Chater, Gilly Ruben, Rupert Edwards, Jamie Marshall and Jenny Zamit.

Special thanks to John Chater and Gilly Ruben for the photographs.

ben hamper
rivethead
tales from the assembly line

Also published by Fourth Estate
Price £7.99